The Seven-Day Financial Makeover is an exceptionally practical guide to transforming your financial future. Its biblical approach and application are supported by worksheets and other useful tools to put you on the right path. You will be amazed at how the tools will help you develop new patterns in your life and allow you to accomplish your family's financial goals and objectives. In my 35-year career in finance, I have never seen a more practical book on personal finances. I recommend it to all!

John C. Mulder
President, WaterStone
Colorado Springs, Colorado

The Seven-Day Financial Makeover is a simple and practical guide for all who need help planning their personal finances. Eric Hoogstra provides many practical examples in the book that help the layperson understand basic financial concepts and overcome common financial problems of today. He entwines biblical messages with his practical guide for a seven-step process to transform your personal financial condition. I recommend this book highly for all.

Sridhar Sundaram, Ph.D.
Chair, Finance Department
Grand Valley State University

Eric Hoogstra draws on his financial experience and God's principles to craft a wonderfully practical, easy-to-read and apply series of action steps you can use to rethink and remake your bank account. This book will be one of the best investments you ever make.

Rex M. Rogers, Ph.D.
President SAT-7®

This is a blueprint to help any family establish a sound financial plan — it's proven, easy to follow, and filled with wisdom.

D. J. Young
Author, speaker, and founder of Wisdom4Dads

If you want to close the hole in your pocket through which all of your money drains, you need this book. Dr. Hoogstra maps out for the reader a realistic, one-week "Roadmap" to "finding financial peace and long-term contentment" and stopping the financial drain. He moves us from being a slave to money to using it as a tool to accomplish God's plan for our lives.

Dr. Rich Rollins
Co-author of *Spiritual Fitness: A Guide to Biblical Maturity*

"Who has time for financial discipline? Now you do! This is such an easy and thorough way to restructure your finances. Start today and you will have a complete plan in seven days!"

Jane H. Hubbard
Director of Organizational Effectiveness (retired)
Delta Air Lines

In *The Seven-day Financial Makeover*, Dr. Hoogstra identifies the major roadblocks that so many people face in their personal finances. But unlike other books on how to deal with your finances, he presents not only the causes of these difficulties, but "action steps" for how to gain victory over your personal finances. What is unique about this approach to financial planning is Dr. Hoogstra's spot-on advice about family budgets, home purchases, credit card debt, investment options, inheritance, and God's perspective on all of these matters. *The Seven-Day Financial Makeover* is a must-read for anyone seeking to gain control of their financial future, with the Lord's perspective in mind. The wisdom contained in this book is as ancient as the Bible and as current as today's marketplace.

Denny Cherette, Founding Partner
Investment Property Associates, LLC

If ever there was a time when people are looking for solid, sensible direction in the management of their finances, this is it. This book does not offer any "quick fixes" or "easy money," but instead provides practical, established principles that are timeless and relevant. I commend Eric Hoogstra's work and am confident that it will make a positive contribution for anyone seeking to build a firm financial foundation.

Dr. Paul Hontz, Senior Pastor
Central Wesleyan Church

I have always believed a person can implement a great financial management plan in short order. Dr. Eric Hoogstra proves this to be true in this very practical seven-day guide to financial health.

Todd Gould
Founder of www.stressfreefinance.com
Author of *Stress-Free Finances*

Great benefits will come to those willing to work through "The Seven-Day Financial Makeover" as provided in Eric Hoogstra' book. His advice is trustworthy and doable! I encourage Christian leaders to get this book and provide it to the many families who now face financial crisis. Can a person's financial situation really be changed for the better in seven days? Absolutely! Apply Dr. Hoogstra's new book and find out.

Jim Lacy, MA, MRE, DMin
Founder, Intentional Interim Church Ministries
Interim District Executive Minister, Converge, Michigan

Of all the things we have learned recently, it has become clear that the way we see and manage money is of major importance. My friend Eric has compiled some great advice that is both wise and practical. Money matters! Which is why this book matters!

Joseph M. Stowell, President
Cornerstone University

The Seven-Day Financial Makeover is a comprehensive guide to gaining control of personal or family finances from a biblical perspective. Practical examples, selected Scripture, and worksheets aid in implementing the defined steps to financial freedom. Eric draws from his personal faith and professional experience to present an easy-to-understand approach for Christians to live within our means, while trusting God to provide for our needs.

Daniel L. Niswander, President/CEO
InfoPower, Inc.

Hoogstra's book is like a GPS for personal finance. It will get you on the right road and help you stay there—sage advice regardless of your age or income. The key for me was Hoogstra's use of the biblical concept of contentment—his book is a lifeline for the "slippery slope of consumption, frustration, and financial bondage."

Gary Gerds, Vice President and General Manager
Grabber, Inc.

Eric Hoogstra is an expert. He not only knows finances, but he knows human nature and our tendency to prolong making the changes necessary to positively impact our financial picture. With wisdom drawn from the pages of Scripture, Eric applies the timeless truths of God's Word in the context of the 21st-century financial landscape. If you're tired of always doing what you've always done and getting the same results—let me commend to you Dr. Hoogstra's *The Seven-Day Financial Makeover* as a way to transform your financial future.

Darryl Bartlett, Executive Director
Holland Rescue Mission

For anyone who wants to clearly understand their personal financial condition from the standpoint of God's call to biblical stewardship, Dr. Eric Hoogstra's *The Seven-Day Financial Makeover* is a must-read. In a series of Daily Action Steps, easy-to-use worksheets, real-life practical applications, and Web resources, Hoogstra provides straightforward tools to develop a habit of financial self-discipline. He systematically applies Scriptural truth to help the reader take control of their monthly budget and personal spending, set goals, invest wisely, and plan for the future. In today's recessionary economy, many will find this book the key to establishing a step-by-step action plan to financial security.

David Pray, President/CEO
Decker Construction, Inc. Grand Rapids, Michigan

This should be a mandatory graduation gift to all college students or a mandatory course before graduation.

Bill Lada, President
World Trade Council of Chicago

After years of study in finances, counseling experience with clients, and doing business himself, Eric has compiled a unique book that will give you the best of what he has learned. This is someone who lives this, not just someone who talks it. I have deep respect for Eric and the commitment he has made toward helping others learn the value of good money management. God is honored when you use what he has given you wisely.

David Muma, Owner
Century Driving School

This book and a one week commitment will lay a firm foundation for effective financial stewardship that can transform your life.

Brett A. Elder, Executive Editor
NIV Stewardship Study Bible

Jesus had a lot to teach us about how to use our money and possessions—in fact, more than all of His teachings on heaven and hell combined. In this short book, Dr. Eric Hoogstra presents practical, down-to-earth advice for every person who wants to be a responsible steward of the financial resources God has provided. For all of us who want to transform our financial future, here is a good place to begin.

Dave Stravers, President
Mission India

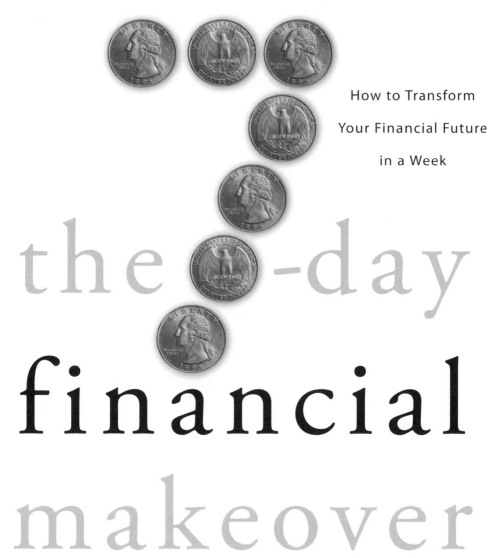

How to Transform
Your Financial Future
in a Week

the 7-day

financial

makeover

Eric J. Hoogstra

credo
house publishers

The Seven-Day Financial Makeover:
How to Transform Your Financial Future in a Week

Copyright © 2010 by Eric J. Hoogstra. All rights reserved.

Published by Credo House Publishers, a division of Credo Communications, LLC, Grand Rapids, Michigan; www.credocommunications.net.

ISBN-10: 1-935391-36-4
ISBN-13: 978-1-935391-36-4

Scripture is taken from the HOLY BIBLE, NEW INTERNATIONAL VERSION®. NIV®. Copyright © 1973, 1978, 1984 by International Bible Society. Used by permission of Zondervan. All rights reserved.

Cover design: Frank Gutbrod
Interior design: Frank Gutbrod

Names and other details have been changed in order to protect the privacy of the individuals whose stories are told in this book.

Printed in the United States of America

This book is dedicated to my mother, Mary Hoogstra,
who taught me how to manage money wisely,
who was a good example,
and who taught me the importance of giving charitably.

contents

Promise: Imagine the relief, contentment, energy, and empowerment you'll feel a week from now. Why wait? This book will show you how to transform your financial future in seven days. Guaranteed!

Introduction xi
Why This Book? xv
Day 1: Assessing Your Current Financial Status 1
Day 2: Understanding the Perspective of Ownership 17
Day 3: Changing Your Financial Status 39
Day 4: Eliminating Life's Budget Busters 73
Day 5: Setting Goals 97
Day 6: Investing to Meet Your Goals 129
Day 7: Planning for Your Future 153
Appendices 167
Book Group Discussion Questions 185
Internet Resources 195
About the Author 197

. . . .

introduction

If someone asked you today about your current financial situation, what would you say? If you're a typical American, you might reply in one or more of the following ways:

- You are worried about your current financial situation.
- You are frustrated that you are working harder and harder, yet getting farther and farther behind with your bills and payments.
- Your growing credit card debt gives you a sense of hopelessness.
- Your home equity loan or second mortgage application has been turned down by yet another bank.
- You are meeting your current payments, but are worried about some of the longer term issues of college planning for the children or the costs of retirement for you.
- You think you are on the right track financially, but you want to be sure.

- You are continually receiving financial statements from your company's 401(k), but you have no idea what they mean or which investment options you should choose.
- You are looking for some direction with your finances.
- You are looking to make changes with your finances that are more in line with biblical principles.
- You have no financial problems, have always lived on a budget, and yet are a financial junkie looking to continue to learn more in this area.

Whatever your circumstances, you picked up this book for a reason. It is probably due to experiencing some difficulties in this aspect of your life.

If you are struggling with financial problems, you have to understand four realities upfront. First, you are not the only one experiencing such problems. If you talk to your friends and acquaintances, you will find many others facing similar concerns.

Second, financial problems are not a normal part of life. If you so desire, you can greatly change your direction and situation. If you are one of those people who want to take action and move toward financial freedom, then this book has been written for you!

Third, this book is designed to help you assess your financial situation and then guide you in making lifelong changes to become more financially secure.

Finally, this book was written to train you to manage your finances so you can be a responsible steward of the financial resources God has provided and entrusted to you. Regardless of your current situation or the depth of your financial problems, this book will enable you to effectively manage your resources from here on out.

Each of our financial stories and situations is unique, and each personal financial situation will require a different set of solutions to solve those issues.

As you continue through this book, you will find I am not providing a one-size-fits-all approach. Instead, I will give you the tools for exploring various options and allow you to develop your own individual plan. That plan will help you find and fulfill God's calling for this important area of life.

A word of encouragement. As we move through this process, we can all be assured that God has called us to trust Him, and He has promised to provide for all of our needs! Unfortunately, many of us have moved away from this eternal dependence on God and relied more on our own skills and abilities, living our lives in a self-centered pattern that often negates the trust we need to have in God. Much of this self-reliance is brought about by the prosperity many of us have experienced in this world, and the individual successes we have achieved using the abilities God has given to us.

In addition, this book is not only designed to help you access your current financial situation, but it will also give you the tools you need to move much more quickly toward the goal of financial freedom. You have the ability to move toward freedom this week if you take responsible and purposeful actions. As you move closer to this goal each day, you will substantially reduce the stresses and financial pressures that plague your life, and greatly increase your peace and contentment. In fact, increased contentment may be even more beneficial than reduced stress.

Remember, God has a specific plan for each of us. As we increasingly follow His guidance, He will bless us. For some, this may sound more like a far-off dream than a probability. Yet with the help of God all things are not only possible, but they also can be achieved!

why this particular book?

This book is different from the stacks of financial self-help or get-rich-quick books that have been written by a number of good and even great authors. Most of these books help us get out of debt or help us invest, but they don't provide a roadmap to show us how to move from our current situation to one of financial peace and long-term contentment. This kind of contentment can come only from God performing His good work in and through our lives. Still, this book will give you the information you need concerning investments and current financial markets.

This book is designed to be read and used over a period of seven days. Your completion of the steps outlined in this book may take a week or longer. Regardless, I guarantee the journey will be worth the effort!

. . . .

The Current State of Personal Finances in America Today

The state of personal finances in America has changed dramatically from that of past generations. In fact, based on some statistics from Crown Financial Ministries:

- Almost half of all Americans spend more per year than they earn.
- Money management is the #1 source of marital conflict today. In fact, 90 percent of divorces today point to financial issues as one of the primary causes.
- The average American carries a credit card balance of more than $9,000 (this figure tends to go up by about a $1,000 per year, and it normally happens around Christmas time).
- More than $800 billion is owed on credit cards today.
- Money mismanagement and lack of a budget causes the average American to use an ATM machine to obtain cash about every other day.
- More money is spent on gambling than on groceries. This trap has caused many of us to base our financial futures on luck or chance.
- Personal bankruptcy rates have grown exponentially in recent years.
- The number of home foreclosures has jumped dramatically. While this increase in the number of foreclosures alone may not be a concern, a number of people are renting homes from landlords who face possible foreclosure, which, in turn, will cause renters to lose their homes in the process.

As you consider these findings, it is important to keep in mind that many Americans are probably in worse financial shape than you are. Many individuals and families today face severe financial difficulties, even if most do not talk about it. This creates a sense of hopelessness for those who incorrectly believe they are the only ones in financial distress. This belief is flat wrong!

When you openly discuss your finances with others, you will find that many have the same problems you do or worse. By sharing and working together, you can support and hold each other accountable as you seek to change your financial future.

. . . .

"Why Didn't I Know This Already?"

Many individuals feel the financial condition they are in is the result of the lack of certain financial skills. One question often asked of me by many in the seminars I conduct is, "Why didn't I know this already?" or "Why was I never taught this in school?" To be honest, these are excellent questions to which I don't have good answers.

In Michigan, where I reside, the state now requires that each student take advanced math courses as part of his or her required curriculum. Michigan still does not require students to take any personal finance courses, however, or even teach students how to balance a checkbook. In fact, one can earn a Ph.D. from a reputable university without learning basic personal financial management skills.

So, where do people learn how to manage their finances today? Unfortunately, most of this training is the responsibility of parents and society. However, most parents also missed much of this training and therefore may not be a good source of such information.

PRACTICAL EXAMPLE

Many researchers are watching the changing behavior of the Baby Boomer generation. These individuals represent almost one-third of America's adult population. Historically, Baby Boomers have been responsible for the development and growth of a number of businesses (including McDonalds), but, as they grow older, their spending patterns are changing. These changes in spending patterns have caused many businesses to rethink their business models. In addition, many of these Boomers have not prepared for and saved enough for retirement. As the balances of Social Security go down, it will be interesting to watch how this group readjusts their lifestyles within the realities that retirement may provide for them.

Society's guidance, based upon its emphasis on constant consumption, constant advertising, and multiple credit card offers, also may not be an acceptable source of proper information concerning personal finance.

So, where should we go for a reliable, trustworthy source of financial guidance? It may surprise you that one of the best sources is the Bible, the inspired Word of God.

. . . .

Biblical Perspectives on Personal Finance

I am constantly amazed by the number of biblical passages that give us exceptional guidance in managing our finances today. All told, more than 2,500 verses in Scripture deal with money and can be used to manage our financial resources. In addition, about two-thirds of Jesus' parables deal with the topic of finances.

Not surprisingly, God clearly understands that people in every generation face financial difficulties, and need rock-solid principles to guide them. Unfortunately, many never take the time to consult the Bible. Either we are worrying about our financial situation or we're working long hours to maintain our current financial lifestyle.

Throughout upcoming sections, this book will use Scripture passages to shed light on God's unlimited knowledge and wisdom concerning the financial topics we will be covering. Scripture will not simply give us a "second opinion," but will be an invaluable reference tool.

. . . .

Can You Change Your Financial Future?

At this point you may be asking yourself, *Can I really change my finances and my financial future?* Thankfully, this frequently asked question can be answered with a resounding "Yes!" At this point you may see problems and despair. Within seven days, I want to instill in you a new vision of confidence, hope, and destiny.

PRACTICAL EXAMPLE

Steve and Bethany have seven children. Steve was earning a salary of $25,000 per year and Bethany was a stay-at-home mom. Over the years, they accumulated more than $40,000 in credit card debt. Through prayer, study, commitment, and changes in their lifestyle, they eliminated all of their debt within five years. They credit the workings of God within their lives for accomplishing so much in such a relatively brief period of time.

I often compare personal finance with personal weight loss: you just need to do the math. If you are eating 3,000 calories per day, which is about 500 calories per day more than you are expending, you will gain one pound every seven days. If you cut your daily calorie intake by 500 calories or 16.7 percent, you will simply break even. If you want to lose weight, you need to eat less than 2,500 calories or exercise more to expend more calories. If you reduce another 500 calories from your diet, a total reduction of one-third of your previous intake, it will take seven days to lose one pound. Keep it up for six months and you'll lose 26 pounds.

As with weight loss, our personal finances may require us to make cuts in our spending (eating less) or to take on additional jobs to earn more (exercise).

As with weight loss, there is no "magic pill" or secret solution to get our finances back on track. The last thing we want to do is go from one diet (budgeting system) to another. Instead, we need to change our behavior. There is no secret formula to make all of your financial problems go away. Unfortunately, I cannot wave a magic wand and cause your financial problems to disappear. Changing your financial situation will take time, effort, and dedication on your part. Many people take several years to dramatically change their financial condition, but my clients always say they would do it again thanks to the many benefits they now enjoy.

PRACTICAL EXAMPLE

Ryan and Beth currently have $5,000 in credit card debt. They have two options for paying this debt: (1) pay a minimal amount of $75 per month, or (2) cut back on some of their expenses and pay $150 toward this debt. If they make the minimum payments, it will take 283 months to pay off this debt at a total cost of $21,225. If Ryan and Beth pay $150 per month, however, they can eliminate this debt in 45.5 months at a total cost of only $6,825. Overall, option 2 would save $14,400 and give them the joys of financial freedom almost 20 years faster than option 1.

PRACTICAL EXAMPLE

Ben and Myra Smith want to take a vacation, and have determined they could put aside $50 per month for the $3,000 cruise of their dreams. If they decide to take the trip now (they saw the credit card advertisements, after all, and discovered they deserve one), it will take them 146 months (more than 12 years at 18 percent) to pay for that wonderful but brief vacation. If they save up for the cruise, however, Ben and Myra will be able to go on one fully paid in only 48 months (4 years) if they earn 10 percent on their saved money. That's a difference of more than 8 years, time enough to save for two more $3,000 luxury cruises. Their motto: Save now to have more fun later!

Individuals and couples I have worked with make significant progress toward their financial goals within a few years, and eventually become debt-free. Therefore, regardless of your current situation, I can assure you there is hope! I can further assure you that the time you spend working though this seven-day money makeover will be both life-changing and well worth the effort!

. . . .

Skills Necessary to Be Successful

Many individuals falsely believe they are "numerically challenged" or do not have the necessary mathematical or financial skills to balance their checkbook or invest for the future effectively. As a result, they create needless chaos for themselves and others.

PRACTICAL EXAMPLE

Some people maintain three or four checking accounts. Each month they use one of them to deposit their paychecks and write their checks. As they do not understand how to balance their checking accounts, after the end of the month they begin using another account. They rotate through these accounts. When it comes time to use an account again, they call the bank and enter the banks' balance as the starting balance. Talk about a juggling act!

In reality, managing your financial resources is a relatively simple process. It certainly does not require using any high level mathematics. You only need to have the basic skills for addition, subtraction, multiplication, and division.

More important than numerical skills, you must be prudent in managing the resources God provides. All it takes is an honest willingness to make some behavioral changes so you don't spend more than you make.

If we need relatively few skills to manage our finances properly, why do so many people have financial issues and problems? One of the reasons is the "I want it now" attitude we all possess thanks to years of marketing and advertising, which have conditioned us to get it now and pay later.

Thankfully, over the next week you can reverse your thinking, make positive changes in your life, and enjoy the satisfaction that comes from using your money wisely.

. . . .

Working with a Group

I cannot overstate the benefits of working through this book with others. Although you may feel uncomfortable sharing some of your family's financial specifics, you'll benefit greatly if you work with others and ask them to hold you accountable.

Toward that end, I have included a number of group discussion questions in the back of this book. Be sure to use them to help guide your discussions.

. . . .

Format for the Remainder of This Book

Over the next seven days, I will present a relatively simple and understandable process.

The first day we will investigate and assess your current financial status. During this part of the journey, we will take time to record all of your income and expenditures in order to identify some of the financial problem areas you may have.

The second day we'll establish the foundation and framework for us to begin to use our finances in an appropriate and biblical manner.

The third day we will begin to explore options and tools for you to consider as you begin to identify the changes you would like to make in your life. These changes will allow you to move from your current financial situation to the life you want to live.

The fourth day we will see how ongoing problems could derail any successful plan.

The fifth day we will begin to explore a new vision for your future by helping you develop goals within a number of important life areas.

The sixth day we will consider a number of options and strategies for investments. This section will become increasingly important as you begin to eliminate debt and begin investing to meet the goals you have established.

The seventh day will focus on longer-term issues we all need to consider, including purchasing life insurance and creating effective wills and trusts.

All of this may seem a bit overwhelming at this point. However, this is a journey we will take together. I'll be glad to serve as your financial guide each step along the way. To avoid feeling overwhelmed, take things one day a time. Be sure to fully complete the work of the day before moving on to the next section.

All along the way, I will share plenty of stories and words of encouragement with you. Believe me, you can change your financial future. Let's begin this exciting journey together!

Action Steps for Today

- Begin by talking with several other people about their finances today. See how many share financial problems similar to yours.
- Make the commitment to complete this life-transforming journey by signing the following pledge:

I want to experience a seven-day money makeover and agree to complete all of the reading, exercises, and worksheets for Days 1 to 7.

_____   _____

Signature   Signature of Spouse or Partner

_____   _____

Date   Date

. . . .

assessing your current financial status

In the Introduction, I asked you a simple question: How do you perceive your current financial condition? Many individuals believe their financial situation is bad, but don't know the true magnitude of their problems. This misperception causes them to incorrectly believe they can manage things when in reality they are on a collision course with financial disaster.

Just being able to pay all of your current bills on time is not necessarily a sign of financial stability. You may still be missing some of your longer-term needs and goals such as saving for retirement or saving for your children's education.

Then again, consistently not being able to pay your bills on time usually signifies significant problems with your finances. The constant pressure of having to select which bills will be paid this week or this month causes stress both in our personal lives and within our relationships, including our relationships with those we love the most. As well, by focusing on these short-term problems we often ignore our God-given priorities, frequently miss the larger picture of life, and too often neglect our own longer-term goals. In short, having financial problems causes undue stress, negatively affects relationships, and also causes some to irreparably put off questions or concerns related to their eternal destiny.

This chapter was designed and written to guide you through a series of simple but important steps. These steps will allow you (and your spouse or partner) to assess your current financial situation.

Today you will begin by determining your periodic variable expenses, your household incomes, and your reoccurring monthly expenses. After you have identified these amounts, you will identify your current level of assets and debts and then determine your personal net worth.

These steps are some of the most important you will take in this seven-day journey, and therefore will take a bit more time than future steps. Still, it is important that you work through today's exercises accurately, honestly, and openly.

Watch out for needless disappointment or frustration as you work through these first steps. No matter how hard you try, you cannot change the past and it's a waste of time to assign blame. Instead, you need to make a commitment to move forward toward a better, more rewarding future.

For most Americans, the completion of today's steps will be sobering since the majority of individuals and couples spend more than they make. In addition, the average person's credit card balance tops $9,000. That said, don't forget you are not alone, and many of your friends and neighbors are in the same position.

When you look at your neighbors and wonder, "How can they afford that…," the truth is, most likely, they can't. There will be a day of reckoning for them, too. You may have tried to "keep up with the Joneses" and found out first-hand that this path leads to financial despair.

So, as you walk through these first few steps, be encouraged that this is the beginning of a journey that will ultimately lead to complete and total financial freedom. What a joy that will be! Ready? Let's begin this process together!

. . . .

Knowing Your Financial Condition in Six Easy Steps

The six steps we will walk through today, although relatively simple to complete, will reveal quite a bit about your current financial condition. The six steps include identifying the variable income and expenses of your household, preparing a projected monthly statement, verifying your monthly expenses, prepare a listing of your personal assets, compiling a comprehensive list of all current debts, and preparing a set of personal financial statements.

These six steps for Day 1 may seem a bit overwhelming, and you may feel you don't have the necessary skills to complete the worksheets on your own. However, the only skills required are basic addition and subtraction skills, along with knowledge of how to fill in boxes on various forms. Please be assured that you have all the skills required to complete these exercises. Taking them one step at a time will make their completion more manageable.

Let's start working through the tasks together.

. . . .

Step One –
Identification of Variable Income and Expenses

The first step is identifying your household's variable income and expenses. It is relatively easy to identify a household's reoccurring income and expenses. It is more difficult to identify income and expenses that occur only one or more times per year.

Examples of variable income include bonuses received at work and tax refunds. The average American receives an annual refund of approximately $2,700. Most individuals use these refunds to catch up on overdue bills, make additional payments toward debt reduction, or even make one-time annual splurges on clothing or other larger purchases. The sad part is that, while people receive this refund after their annual tax return is filed, they often pay extra to receive it in an expedited manner. These overpayments are interest-free loans to the government. Instead, make the necessary changes to receive more take-home pay each month, which will help you balance your monthly budget.

Examples of variable expenses include automobile insurance and Christmas presents. The average household spends $1,000 for Christmas presents each year. If you broke this down into a regular expense, you would need to budget $83 per month, more than most people can probably afford. So, where are these funds coming from? In most cases they're coming from increasing debt, primarily through the use of credit cards.

TRANSFORMATIONAL TIP

Many Americans purchase Christmas presents assuming they will have the money in January to pay these bills. However, when one looks at all of the other expenses during the holidays, this payoff rarely occurs and households begin the year already further behind financially. Instead, make plans to enjoy Christmas more while spending less.

In the case of automobile insurance, one often pays these expenses in advance for the next six months. If one does not plan for these semi-annual expenses, it may be difficult to find the funds necessary to pay for these periodic bills.

Okay, let's find out how you're doing. In the back of this book, use Worksheet 1 to list all of your variable income and expenses. Then compute the monthly amounts we will use in Step Two.

It is important to take the time to complete this step fully before moving on as the accuracy of your next step will be directly related to your accuracy with this step. If you are married, spend some time with your spouse to complete this exercise. If you are single, you may want to ask someone to help you during this process, and to serve as an accountability partner.

As you list future variable expenses, you may not know exactly how much you are going to spend on this year's vacation or this year's Christmas presents. If that's the case, you may want to look back at last year's expenses as guides for determining what you might spend this year.

In order to substantially reduce the stresses and financial pressures that plague your life and greatly increase your peace and contentment, stop reading and complete Step One. Believe me, you'll be so glad you did! After all, you're beginning an exciting, transformative journey!

PRACTICAL EXAMPLE

Bill and Mary Smith spend on average $600 for Christmas presents in December, $200 for back to school items in August, $300 for dentists in November, $100 for birthday presents in March, and $1,200 for a family vacation in June. In addition, the Smiths pay $1,150 for property taxes in September, and $50 more for property taxes in February. The total amount of all of these variable expenses is $3,600 per year. To cover all of these items, the Smiths will need to factor $300 into their monthly budgets.

. . . .

Step Two –
Completion of a Projected Monthly Statement

The second step is identifying your regular and reoccurring monthly income and expenses. To enable you to do this, use Worksheet 2 in the back of this book. This worksheet includes a number of income and expense categories and subcategories. It is important that you enter these amounts as accurately as possible. Again, asking a spouse or friend to work with you may be helpful.

As you complete Step Two, be sure to report your actual incomes and expenses. Don't report what you would like them to be, or what you hope they will be after making some adjustments, or what might be the case after you receive that new position at work.

To increase the accuracy of your figures, you may want to go back a few months in your financial records and compute month averages. Of course, a number of expenses will be easy to compute, including one's mortgage or car payment. More variable expenses such as food, entertainment, and recreation will be accurate only if you average your actual expenses over the past few months. If you are still unsure what to report in a given category, use your best guess. Then again, for some categories you'll simply enter zero.

The goal of Step Two is to prepare a financial statement that shows your typical monthly cash inflow and outflow. This important step often results in one or more "Aha!" moments.

PRACTICAL EXAMPLE

Mike and Sharron Brock, along with their three children, live a relatively simple life. Mike and Sharron each make $3,000 per month, and, after taxes, take home a joint income of approximately $4,500. Their major expenses include $1,500 for their mortgage, $800 for two car lease payments and fuel, $200 for insurance, $500 for food, $150 for cable and cell phones, $200 for utilities, $200 for entertainment, and $750 per month in childcare for their three children. Based on these numbers, while their monthly income is $4,500, their expenses also total $4,500 per month, leaving them no monthly surplus. Still, Mike would like to upgrade their cable service and take the family on vacation next year. Sharron would like to start putting money away for retirement. Based on their current level of spending, however, the Brocks cannot do any additional spending without going into debt. In addition, they cannot build any savings in case an appliance breaks or their cars need repairs. Even though they are able to pay their current bills, this couple needs to make some spending cuts in order to better position themselves for the future.

If you live in a two-income household, it's fascinating to identify the income generated by each spouse, and then to record both the income and work-related expenses of the lower income spouse on a separate sheet.

Throughout the past 25 years, I have talked with many two-income couples who claim one would love to stay at home while the children are young, but then insist it's impossible because of all of their financial needs.

By removing all of the extra expenses for a two-income household—including having two cars, one's business wardrobe, daycare for the children, and prepared meals—the net income of a dual income household usually is much less than they would have guessed.

When one computes the true net earnings for each spouse, the lower income spouse often works for only a dollar or two an hour. As a result, making the change to a single income family is usually not difficult.

(Note: If you are interested in exploring this option, you may want to log onto Amazon and purchase a used copy of *Women Leaving the Workplace: How to Make the Transition from Work to Home* by Larry Burkett. This is a book I highly recommend.)

Those who receive variable income, including commissioned salespersons, often find it difficult to determine their average monthly income. To begin, take your W-2 income for the past year and divide it by 12 to compute a monthly average.

Of course, this year's projected earnings, based upon last year's averages, will be only as accurate as this year's monthly incomes are similar to last year's. One must continually watch his or her earnings trends and make monthly or quarterly comparisons with past years. If your income so far this year is significantly lower than last year, you need to make corresponding adjustments to this year's income statement and related expenses.

Whatever you do, be careful during good times. Don't make the mistake so many Americans made during the middle of this decade. Absolutely refuse to adopt a "this will never change" attitude and certainly don't allow your standard of living to exceed what your "normal" average earnings can support. Otherwise, the next economic downturn will trip you up and force you to significantly lower your standard of living.

PRACTICAL EXAMPLE

Bob Johnson is a mortgage broker with ABC Mortgage and receives commissions only based on his performance. Bob made $2,000 last month, and $6,000 the month before that. During the first quarter of last year Bob's income topped $25,000, but his annual income came in close to $72,000. During the first quarter of this year his total income was $18,000, or a decrease of 28 percent from last year. As a result, Bob should start budgeting at an income level that's 72 percent of what he made last year, and reduce his expenses accordingly.

After you have entered amounts into the various income and expense categories on Worksheet 2, add everything up. Then subtract your expenses from your income to arrive at an accurate picture of how you're doing.

If your worksheet says you have a monthly surplus, you may be quite proud of yourself. When working with individuals and couples in this situation, however, I often ask them a basic question: "Are you telling me that at the end of each month you always have money that you don't know what to do with?"

The response I usually get is they not only don't have any surplus funds at month's end, but they're consistently falling short.

If this is true of you, go back over the facts and figures you listed on Worksheet 2. What figures need to be double-checked? What facts did you forget to list? Among other things, how much "petty cash" do you put in your wallet or purse each week? What unrecorded expenses are listed on your monthly credit card statements the past three months? Even small things like your daily latte, mocha, or cappuccino can add $100 or more every month.

If you are in a deficit situation, don't forget you are not alone. Most households overspend on a regular basis. If you could look closely at the financial records of individuals you believe are wealthy, you probably would discover they are simply using higher amounts of debt than you. The true millionaires are average people who enjoy a simple, but contented, lifestyle.

Again, it is important that you have a good handle on your monthly expenses before moving to Step Three. Reading about these concepts without doing Worksheet 2 will do nothing to change your financial future. Then again, you could start saving thousands of dollars between now and New Years. Go for it!

. . . .

Step Three –
Verifying the Monthly Income and Expenses

The figures you listed on Worksheet 2 may not be entirely accurate. So, while you continue working through all of the steps in this book, begin keeping a record of all the expenses you have. After you finish this week, keep recording your expenses for another 24 days. It may sound like a lot of busy work, but you'll be so glad you didn't skip this step.

Within the next month, you'll probably discover a few things you need to add or correct to make Worksheet 2 more accurate. Along the way, you also may discover a few spending habits you didn't know you (and your spouse) have. Resist the temptation to assign blame. Instead, congratulate yourself for going the extra mile!

Later this week, and again next month, you can decide what spending habits you want to change. The more you learn during Step Three, the faster you'll be able to pursue peace of mind and greater financial freedom.

Unlike most steps, this one is ongoing. So take two minutes to record any receipts you've received today, and promise yourself that you'll do the same tomorrow.

Then keep moving forward!

. . . .

Step Four –
Listing Your Assets

This is one of the easier steps today: identifying and listing your assets. An asset is anything you own. Assets include such tangible items as your house, your clothes, your jewelry, your cars, your exercise equipment, your music collection, and other possessions that have monetary value. Assets also include such intangible items as bank, savings, retirement, and investment accounts.

Use Worksheet 3 as a guide to identify all of your assets and their current value. The estimated value of some of your larger assets, including your house, may be fairly easy to determine. But many smaller dollar figures you list will be educated guesses. Don't think rock-bottom garage sale prices for smaller items. Instead, determine what you probably could get for the item on eBay. In every case, list what the current value is, not what you paid for the item.

Normally, you would list the assets on this worksheet by their relative liquidity including the most liquid of all assets, your personal checking and savings accounts. Items you would not include on this worksheet include leased vehicles and term life insurance policies, since neither is a form of ownership.

If you have a whole life or universal life insurance policy, you can include the cash value of each policy as an asset. If you aren't sure of what the cash value is, you may want to contact the life insurance agent who sold you the policy.

As you list your assets, please remember that vehicles depreciate quickly, and in some cases you may owe more than the car is worth. The same may be true for your house. But don't factor in what you owe. Simply list their resale value in today's market.

When you have listed all of your assets, total them, smile, take a quick stretch break, and then proceed to the next step.

. . . .

Step Five –
Preparing a List of Current Debts

This step isn't quite as fun, but it's definitely the easiest. Use Worksheet 4 to list all of the individuals and companies to whom you owe money, including the actual amount owed and the interest rate being charged.

Examples include credit card debt, car loans, unpaid medical bills, student loans, property taxes, home loans, second mortgages and home equity lines of credit. If you are unsure of the amount you owe, or the interest rate you're being charged, call the bank or company or look up your account online.

After you've finished compiling all the facts and figures, you may want to rewrite the list on a new worksheet. This time, list all of your debts from highest to lowest interest rate. This prioritized list will be invaluable later this week.

PRACTICAL EXAMPLE

Let's say you have three debts: a $70,000 mortgage at 7%, a $5,000 credit card debt at 23%, and a $2,000 department store debt at 15%. On the worksheet, you would list the mortgage first as it has the lowest interest rate, even though the department store has the lowest balance. However, when it comes time to pay them off, you would select the one with the lowest balance as the one to pay off first.

TRANSFORMATIONAL TIP

If you have an overwhelming amount of debt, don't let false guilt, past hurt, or depression immobilize you. Recently I counseled a couple who listed debts to more than 150 different individuals, couples, and businesses. Almost 100 of the debts could have been satisfied with $1,000. The couple had considered bankruptcy but, due to personal religious beliefs, could not bring themselves to file. Doing nothing doesn't work. You owe it to yourself to keep moving forward. Before this week's over you will have a realistic clear-cut plan for reducing your debts, increasing your net worth, and enjoying life more.

. . . .

Step Six –
Preparing a Personal Financial Statement

We're almost done! The next step is integrating some of the key numbers you've compiled today. Start by taking Worksheet 3, which lists your assets, and enter the total amount of debt listed at the end of Worksheet 4. Now subtract that debt from your assets to arrive at your current net worth.

Don't be surprised if your current net worth is low or even negative. Thankfully, you've compiled other information you can use in coming days to substantially improve your net worth over time. Whatever you do, don't toss these worksheets. Instead, hang onto them as reminders of where you started on your journey to financial freedom.

It's almost time to close this book for the day, but not quite yet.

. . . .

Are You Feeling Wealthy?

So, how are you feeling after everything we covered today? Wealthy? Or poor?

To begin to put your current financial situation into perspective, 20 percent of the world's population earns less than $1.00 per day. Another 20 percent earns less than $2.00 per day. On the opposite end of the financial spectrum, only 20 percent of the world's population earns more than $70.00 per day, $490 per week, or $25,480 per year.

Most likely, you are among the top 20 percent of income earners in the world today.

Summary and Application

In many ways, today was the most challenging day of the week. Although a few numbers may be discouraging, they are what they are. Today's exercises should have given you a sense of relief. You now possess both accurate numbers and a true household financial statement.

I'm sure you already have mentally noted possible changes you could make in coming days. I hope that these ideas have made you feel empowered and given you options. Whatever you do, don't give up hope or quit now. I've never seen a financial situation so bad that the individual (or couple) couldn't turn it around.

With God's help, all things are possible. So, let's keep moving forward together!

Action Steps for Today

- Complete Worksheet 1 to determine your variable income and expenses.
- Complete Worksheet 2 to create your projected monthly income statement.
- Verify your monthly income and expense numbers by recording them daily over the next month.
- Begin Worksheet 3 by listing all of your assets.
- Complete Worksheet 4 by listing all of your debts.
- Go back and finish Worksheet 3, which should give you a fairly accurate personal financial statement.

D A Y 2

. . . .

understanding the perspective of ownership

So far in your financial journey we have taken a rather analytical approach to determine your actual current financial status. Now we need to review some of the basic spiritual foundations that will provide significant guidance as we move together though the rest of the week.

Building our financial future on biblical principles is like building our homes on rock instead of sand. If we build our financial future on these biblical principles, God will continue to bless them and us.

The concepts presented today, and the biblical foundation upon which they are based, may be very enlightening to you. Among other things, we want to remember that God is the true owner of all of our possessions, and that we are the stewards or managers of these possessions. If you can agree with these two primary biblical principles, the rest of your journey this week will be rather easy. If you don't agree with them, however, understanding and applying the concepts in the rest of this book could prove a bit more challenging.

The bottom line: If we continue to act as if all of our financial resources belong to us, we will continue to have financial problems. By moving to a more biblical model, we will put our trust for our financial future where it should be—with God alone.

. . . .

God Is the Owner of Everything!

Today we will be covering two of the most important and fundamental principles of Christian financial management and proper financial stewardship: God is the owner of all and we're responsible to act as stewards of the financial resources God provides to us.

Before we cover these concepts in depth, it is important to review some passages in God's Word that give us insight into the concept of the ownership of our possessions.

Let's take a look at a number of passages that declare God owns everything and everything we have comes from God.

The earth is the Lord's, and everything in it (1 Corinthians 10:26).

[Job] said, "Naked I came from my mother's womb, and naked I will depart. The Lord gave and the Lord has taken away; may the name of the Lord be praised" (Job 1:21).

These passages of Scripture make it clear that God is the true owner of all of our possessions and everything else that exists within this world. So what does this mean to us and the management of our money? Everything!

If we trust God will provide all of our daily needs, do we have the faith to allow God to control our finances?

If God owns it all, then anything we have is His and we are only temporary holders of the possessions we have while on earth. God provides us with gifts and blessings, but with these gifts comes the responsibility to manage them in ways that honor God.

Mismanagement of the possessions God has given to us is no different from any other sin against God. Too often we ask God to forgive all our sins, but don't confess or believe that God will forgive our financial mistakes. If we have mismanaged the possessions God has given to us, we need to confess this mismanagement to God. If we confess this sin with all of our heart, God will forgive us as He does any other sins.

Think about this: If God wanted to, could He not change your financial status or remove all of your financial problems? Therefore, if God wants you to confess your sins of financial mismanagement, could He not solve your financial problems after you make this confession to Him?

Over the years, thousands of individuals have symbolically transferred the ownership of all of their possessions to God. Although it's not possible to make such a transfer legally, symbolically transferring them to God changes our attitudes toward possessions, and helps us treat them with respect to their rightful owner. This is an important transfer for all of us to make.

Recognizing that God owns everything, I hereby symbolically transfer ownership of my possessions to God. I promise to manage all of them in a manner that brings honor, glory, and praise to their rightful owner.

_____   _____
Signature   Signature of Spouse or Partner

_____   _____
Date   Date

. . . .

The Concept of Stewardship

If God is the owner of our earthy possessions, it follows that we should be good stewards of them. In the U.S., we have been given an abundance of resources that most other countries of the world can only dream about. Even the poorest person in the U.S. has far more possessions than those in the vast majority of nations. With these valuable resources comes the responsibility of using them in ways their owner desires and prescribes.

The prophet Malachi wrote that those who are wise in the management of their possessions will be given more (3:6-12). This passage also states the opposite: resources will be withheld from those who do not manage them wisely. God does not place resources in "dry holes," so for us to gain the resources we need to move past our financial problems, we need to first manage what we do have in a God-honoring way.

The concept of stewardship over the resources we do have is well documented in passages from both the Gospel of Matthew and the Gospel of Luke:

> "No one can serve two masters. Either he will hate the one and love the other, or he will be devoted to the one and despise the other. You cannot serve both God and Money" (Matthew 6:24; see also Luke 16:13).

> "Whoever can be trusted with very little can also be trusted with much, and whoever is dishonest with very little will also be dishonest with much. So if you have not been trustworthy in handling worldly wealth, who will trust you with true riches? And if you have not been trustworthy with someone else's property, who will give you property of your own?" (Luke 16:10-12).

For us to manage our resources in a God-honoring way, we'll need to do things differently from most of our neighbors, and certainly differently from the way the world wants us to manage them.

The world continually tries to sell us products that supposedly will make us happy. In almost every case, they're not telling the truth. Advertisers spend no less than $200 billion dollars every year to convince Americans to desire "new" or "improved" products we do not need. The minute we buy into their sales pitches, we're discontent with what we already have. That dissatisfaction is not from God!

To change our feelings of discontentment, we need to let the Word of God fill us with the knowledge of proper financial management, and then cause us to be satisfied with the possessions we already have.

PRACTICAL EXAMPLE

When I quote Matthew 6:24, I often end it with "you cannot serve both God and BMW 750i's." But it's not just BMWs. Many of us worship a variety of possessions, either current ones or ones wished for. The concept of idols in today's society is still alive and well!

We all need godly knowledge on how to manage our finances, and the words of the Bible to guide us. Unfortunately, even with free access to the Scriptures, research surveys show little difference between how "average" Christians and most non-Christians handle money. In fact, the overall level of charitable giving by "average" Christians is lower overall compared with most non-Christians.

We have a lot of work ahead of us. For the remainder of the week, let's ask God to correct the attitudes we have toward finances.

Jesus was right: We cannot serve two masters. Which master will you serve in this life?

. . . .

God's Direction for Your Finances

God has a plan for your future. Would you also agree that God has a plan for your financial future? Too often we ask God to give us more when we haven't started properly managing the resources we already have. Yet Jesus was clear:

> "Whoever can be trusted with very little can also be trusted with much, and whoever is dishonest with very little will also be dishonest with much. So if you have not been trustworthy in handling worldly wealth, who will trust you with true riches? And if you have not been trustworthy with someone else's property, who will give you property of your own?" (Luke 16:10-12).

It's good to ask ourselves, "If I am not being faithful with the resources I currently have, why should God add to them?"

So, what does it take to honor God with our possessions?

In changing our perspective of ownership from us to God, we must keep in mind the importance of contentment with what we have, and the power of prayer in the management of our finances.

. . . .

The Importance of Contentment

The importance of contentment is the first factor we must consider in moving toward a God-honoring financial lifestyle. Let's take a look at a few passages from the Bible that deal with this issue:

"But seek first his kingdom and his righteousness, and all these things will be given to you as well. Therefore do not worry about tomorrow, for tomorrow will worry about itself. Each day has enough trouble of its own" (Matthew 6:33-34).

But godliness with contentment is great gain. For we brought nothing into the world, and we can take nothing out of it. But if we have food and clothing, we will be content with that. People who want to get rich fall into temptation and a trap and into many foolish and harmful desires that plunge men into ruin and destruction. For the love of money is a root of all kinds of evil. Some people, eager for money, have wandered from the faith and pierced themselves with many griefs (1 Timothy 6:6-10)

Contentment with what we have is an attitudinal shift anyone can make. It doesn't cost us anything. In fact, it will save us thousands of dollars every year. Being content with what we have is difficult, though, since we're constantly bombarded with the world's philosophy that "more is better" and that "the more we have the more successful and happy we will become."

In addition, when we compare ourselves with others, we often seem to come up short. Of course, we usually compare ourselves only to those who have more, not those who have less. We need to understand that having more will not make us a success, and purchasing even more "stuff" will fuel only temporary happiness at best.

Have you ever purchased something you really wanted, only to discover it left you with an empty feeling inside? *Is this all there is? I thought I would enjoy this more.* We often compensate for such hollow feelings by deciding we need to purchase something else that will make us happy. We're notorious for perpetuating the vicious cycle of relentlessly pursuing happiness by acquiring bigger houses, newer cars, and better toys.

When we believe "more stuff" brings more happiness, we're heading down the slippery slope of consumption, frustration, and financial bondage.

I am consistently amazed by the number of people I work with who outwardly seem to have it all together financially and project a successful image to the community, but who are a financial wreck. Often the people you think are wealthy, based on their conspicuous display of earthly possessions, are in fact living from paycheck to paycheck, often only one paycheck away from bankruptcy. Stop comparing yourself to such people!

PRACTICAL EXAMPLE

Recently I purchased an Apple iPod only to have it become obsolete within the matter of a few months. The next model to hit the market had the ability to surf the Internet and play videos. Thanks to some cool advertising, I decided I wanted this new model. I almost felt like I needed it. Yet when I purchased my original iPod, all I wanted was to listen to my favorite music. The original model was fine for doing this! In the end, I chose to be content with my older model. My commitment to God and my family had won out over their slick advertising.

What is contentment? It's the confidence that what we have is all we need. Americans already have a much higher lifestyle than most of the world. Billions of people cannot even conceive of owning a car, let alone a beautiful home. We all have so much already. If we want to honor God with our possessions, is it really that big of a step to develop an attitude of contentment?

. . . .

Accepting the Provisions of God

One of the fundamental principles in God's Word is that He *will* provide for all of our needs. Of course, there's one condition. Jesus said:

"But seek his kingdom, and these things will be given to you as well" (Luke 12:31).

All God asks is that we trust in him and the blessings he provides. In his first letter to Timothy, Paul says:

Command those who are rich in this present world not to be arrogant nor to put their hope in wealth, which is so uncertain, but to put their hope in God, who richly provides us with everything for our enjoyment (1 Timothy 6:17).

The Scriptures clearly state that if we trust in our personal riches, they will flee from us and disappear. God's blessings, however, are good for all of this life and throughout eternity.

Will all of us be blessed equally in this life? I think the Bible is clear on this point as well. In 1 Samuel we're told:

"The LORD sends poverty and wealth; he humbles and he exalts" (1 Samuel 2:7).

The fact is, we will not be equally wealthy, or have the same number of financial blessings in this life.

At times, I am asked why God is not showering a particular individual with blessings. In some cases, I believe God withholds financial blessings from those who are not being good stewards or managers of the resources that God has given them.

Sometimes, however, I can't understand why some are blessed and others are not, or why some individuals who are doing the will of the Lord still live in financial need while others who disregard God prosper. Some of these concerns will be answered only as we proceed down the road of life, and others won't be answered fully until we enter into the glory of heaven.

Regardless, God intends to bless us so he can channel his blessings through us to others. God wants us to be blessed so we can bless others in turn. If we hoard God's blessings, though, He may decide to withhold further blessings from us.

. . . .

The Importance of Prayer

Beyond contentment, we need to recognize the importance and benefits of prayer. When God wants to get our attention, one of the fastest ways is through our personal finances.

We need to be in prayer for God's guidance in managing our resources, just as we need to pray about other areas of life. With prayer we often come to better understand the will of God. By following God's will, we can more fully manage our resources in a way that pleases him.

. . . .

Developing the Proper Attitude toward Money

Before we can truly change our budget, we need to change our attitudes toward money. Changing our attitudes can be very difficult since money often defines who we believe we are, or who we want others to think we are.

As we begin to look at our resources through the lens of God as owner, however, we'll start to look at those resources differently. Financial resources are no longer about us and what they can do for us. Rather, we begin to thank God for what we have and ask him how to use our existing resources to bless others.

This change of attitude is huge. I'm no longer dependent on acquiring more stuff in order to be happy or satisfied. In fact, I can be more than content. I can also be pleasing to God and a blessing to others. Life doesn't get any better than that!

. . . .

Establishing the Right Balance in Our Lives

Establishing the right balance in our lives is important not only to our physical health, but also to our financial health. Too often we maintain an unhealthy lifestyle by trying to get more and more out of the daily "rat race." We try to keep going and going to be everything to everyone, and end up being nothing to anyone.

Sadly, in our feverish attempts to bless our families by providing a better lifestyle, we can inadvertently harm or damage our family relationships. We can end up hurting those we love if we never have enough time for them.

TRANSFORMATIONAL TIP

As parents, we want an excellent environment in which to raise our children. We also want to give them the things we never had growing up. In order to provide these things, though, are we working too hard? Worse, are we seldom home long enough to spend quality time with our kids? While our kids may enjoy some of the great things we've made available to them, the reality is they would rather spend more time with us. Remember, our children spell "love" t-i-m-e.

Maintaining financial balance is important to our physical health. Too much of the daily pressures of life can lead to being overworked, over-committed, and under undue stress, which in turn can lead to high blood pressure and heart failure. Furthermore, eating on the run in order to be "more productive" leads to unhealthy eating, which causes further health problems.

Striking a balance in the major areas of life—including God, family, health, and work—is difficult at best. Because of our God-given abilities, we often experience significant success in one area of our lives. As a result of that success, we can place a major focus of our time on that one area of life. But doing so only means we'll devote less than enough time to other areas.

Put another way, our drive to be successful in our professional careers can cause us to lose precious time with our family members. Left unbridled, our ambition will drive away our spouse and leave our children feeling neglected and angry.

Later this week we will work on developing goals to find the "right" balance in each area of life. For now, we simply need to recognize what drives us daily, and discover where we have been spending too much of our time.

. . . .

What Is True Financial Freedom?

We have discussed the goal of becoming financially free. However, what does it mean to be financially free? For many, to be financially free means to be debt-free and to have a savings account that allows you to purchase what you want when you want it. Thankfully, that's not the only definition! The ability to have whatever we want may sound good, but it shifts the focus of our finances from God to ourselves. So, it's definitely not the definition God wants us to use.

If we do not adopt God's definition, God may use financial crises to shift our focus back to him. I have always appreciated the definition of financial freedom stated by the late Larry Burkett. He defined financial freedom as (a) the freedom from the bondage of debt and habits that enslave us, and (b) being content with the resources God has already given us.

Equally important, Burkett also defines financial freedom as (c) the freedom to serve God and others, without hesitation, in obedience to the Holy Spirit, and thereby fulfill the purpose for which we were created.

For many individuals, the last part of Burkett's definition is exciting. Yet for others, it is frightening. Here's why. Too often we feel that if we give our finances to God, and give God total control of our lives, he will call us to be missionaries in a desperately poor third world country.

I believe that, while God may want some of us to serve overseas, the United States is one of the largest mission fields today. God very well may want you to remain within your community, serving Him by doing some of the work you are already doing.

As you move toward this more comprehensive view of financial freedom, I hope you will continually look for opportunities to serve God.

This definition of financial freedom is also applicable to retirement. Interestingly, retirement is not discussed in Scripture. I am not saying that retirement is unbiblical, but the idea of us riding off into the sunset to enjoy a life of leisure doesn't appear to be part of God's plan.

God has a purpose for each of us, and we have the opportunity in retirement to find different ways to serve the kingdom of God. Retirement often offers us the freedom to be able to go wherever God calls us and do whatever we can in his service.

Retirement, then, should be seen as a golden opportunity to spend more time serving God and others.

. . . .

Returning to God a Portion of What Is Already His

Most parents reading this book can relate to the idea of taking your kids to a restaurant, paying for the entire meal, and then having one of your children complain bitterly if you take one of their French fries. Or, less than an hour after you have purchased all of the family groceries, to have one of your children complain if you eat one or two of their potato chips.

I believe God often feels this way about us. God continually showers us with blessings, only to watch us complain when He asks us to give a small portion back to him or to others.

. . . .

Earthly Versus Heavenly Treasures

You may have heard the famous question, "Are you placing your faith in the dot or the line?" The dot refers to this life, while the line refers to all of eternity. Some of us get so wrapped up in the day-today struggles of life that we forget our time on earth is but a brief moment, and that eternity is forever.

Before we consider giving, we need to put life and eternity in proper perspective. Consider these famous words of Jesus:

"Do not store up for yourselves treasures on earth, where moth and rust destroy, and where thieves break in and steal. But store up for yourselves treasures in heaven, where moth and rust do not destroy, and where thieves do not break in and steal. For where your treasure is, there your heart will be also" (Matthew 6:19-21).

Jesus, God's Son, warns us not to place our hopes, dreams, and goals in this world, but rather to place all of our treasures in heaven. Of course, if anyone looked at your checking account, he or she would quickly see how you are spending your money. Believe me, it would not take them long to determine where your focus is. It's time to turn our focus on things above.

In his book *The Eternity Portfolio,* Alan Gotthadt asserts that God has only two objectives for money in this life: investing in our family, and investing in others around us. This isn't a new idea, of course.

. . . .

Giving to God throughout History

Giving to God a portion of the resources he has given us is clearly communicated in Scripture. Consider these passages:

The first of the ripe fruits and all the gifts brought to the Lord will go to the priest. The best of all the first fruits and of all your special gifts will belong to the priests. You are to give them the first portion of your ground meal so that a blessing may rest on your household (Ezekiel 44:30).

Each of you must bring a gift in proportion to the way the LORD your God has blessed you (Deuteronomy 16:17).

As you review Scripture, and the basic history of the tithe, you'll find that the tithe is not a spiritual or religious concept. Rather, it's a unit of measure signifying a tenth. During Old Testament time, the Israelites were required to give a tenth of their crops and herds to God. (As well, they were encouraged to give free will offerings, they were required to make sacrifices, and they were instructed to care for the poor, needy, and destitute in their community. Still, everything started with the mandatory tithe.)

Today, many people assume the tithe was an Old Testament requirement, and assume it isn't applicable to us today, even though Jesus talked about it.

Beyond that, Jesus and his apostles had a lot more to say about giving.

He said to them, "Then give to Caesar what is Caesar's, and to God what is God's" (Luke 20:25).

"Give, and it will be given to you. A good measure, pressed down, shaken together and running over, will be poured into your lap. For with the measure you use, it will be measured to you" (Luke 6:38).

Each man should give what he has decided in his heart to give, not reluctantly or under compulsion, for God loves a cheerful giver (2 Corinthians 9:7).

You will be made rich in every way so that you can be generous on every occasion, and through us your generosity will
result in thanksgiving to God (2 Corinthians 9:11).

Command them [Christians] to do good, to be rich in good deeds,
and to be generous and willing to share (1 Timothy 6:18).

In these passages we are clearly called to give generously to God
and others. Several of the passages convey the benefits of generous
giving, echoing what God says in the Hebrew Scriptures. In one of
the most famous passages, God says:

"Bring the whole tithe into the storehouse, that there may be
food in my house. Test me in this," says the LORD almighty,
"and see if I will not throw open the floodgates of heaven
and pour out so much blessing that you will not have room
enough for it" (Malachi 3:10).

It is interesting to note that this particular Bible passage is the
only one in which God calls us to put him to the test. A number of
people have misused this passage, however, in their attempts to increase giving to a church or charitable organization, or in an attempt
to convince us that the more we give, the more we will get.

I believe we need to be careful to not use any Scripture passages
to promote non-biblical theories of prosperity. Those theories ad-
vocate such ungodly ideas as "give to get," or "give to get back a lot
more in return."

The blessings referred to in these passages may not come in the
form of financial returns. Many times God gives us the gifts of contentment, peace, and joy. Still, the Bible is clear that if we give to
God and others, we will receive blessings in return.

So, how many of us are following these giving principles today?

According to research completed by Crown Financial Ministries, a third of all Christians don't give anything; many others say they are tithing, but only 10 percent really do; and the average level of giving is only 2.5 percent of one's income.

This organization further reported that giving has declined significantly over the past decade, and that a third of Christian families struggle to give due to debt and the daily financial pressures of living.

Based on a survey done by the Barna Group, 6 percent all American adults tithe. Then again, 83 percent reported donating an average of 3 percent of their income to charitable agencies. Churches and other places of worship received 65 percent of their donations, but the average amount contributed per donor was 2 percent less than what they gave five years earlier.

The Barna Group determined that most Americans are willing to give more generously than they typically do, but it takes a well-executed approach by a church to encourage greater generosity. Furthermore, Barna identified five reasons why people don't give more: (a) they feel their church doesn't provide a compelling vision for how the money will make a difference in the world, (b) they do not see a sufficient return on their investment, (c) they don't realize their church needs more money to be effective, (d) they're ignorant about what the Bible teaches about money, and (e) they're self-centered.

In addition, some lack of giving is caused by disagreements between spouses, especially if one spouse is not a Christian. Such situations require much wisdom, prayer, and grace. Sometimes a Christian spouse can voluntarily earn extra money and demonstrate the blessings of giving. In some cases, however, a non-Christian spouse can forbid religious giving. In such cases where the non-Christian is the head of the household, the Christian spouse can only pray that his or her spouse will have a change of heart someday.

All things being equal, I challenge you to conduct an experiment over the next six months. Each month give 10 percent of your income to God and trust that He will provide all of your needs. Giving this 10 percent may require some real sacrifices, and you may need to take a number of steps to make your goal every month. But go for it and see what God does!

Of course, I find it humorous whenever someone asks me whether their tithe should be based upon their gross or net income. I reply by asking if they want God's blessings to be gross or net.

People who take this commitment seriously often tell me wonderful stories about how God is changing them and their finances.

One woman's commitment to give 10 percent meant she needed to contribute an additional $50 to her church the very next day. The next morning she wore a coat she hadn't worn for some time. Upon arriving at church, the woman was still unsure of how she would be able to fulfill her commitment. Before hanging up her coat, however the woman checked its pockets and found a $50 bill. She had no idea how it got there, but she certainly knew what to do with it!

In another case, a couple made the commitment to tithe, but they were unsure how they could increase their giving so much. When they balanced their checkbook, however, they discovered several mathematical errors. It turned out the extra money in their account was exactly the amount they needed to give that Sunday.

Again and again, people who have made the commitment to give a tithe for six months have told me they don't want to go back to their old ways. As well, they continue to report more and more benefits of their increased giving. They can see God's good hand at work.

One of the assignments I'll give you at the end of this section is to review your spending and determine what it would take for you to make this level of commitment. It very well may be one of the most important exercises you do all week.

God wants to use you as a channel of His many blessings so you can bless others. Are you willing to be such a channel? I hope so!

. . . .

To Whom Should We Give?

When we're ready to give, where should we give? Again, let's look at God's Word, the Bible, for the answers. Here are two passages we've already considered, but please read them again.

> "Bring the whole tithe into the storehouse, that there may be food in my house. Test me in this," says the LORD Almighty, "and see if I will not throw open the floodgates of heaven and pour out so much blessing that you will not have room enough for it" (Malachi 3:10).

> Command them to do good, to be rich in good deeds, and to be generous and willing to share. In this way they will lay up treasure for themselves as a firm foundation for the coming age, so that they may take hold of the life that is truly life (1 Timothy 6:18-19).

Here's one more passage quoting the words of Jesus:

> "Sell your possessions and give to the poor. Provide purses for yourselves that will not wear out, a treasure in heaven that will not be exhausted, where no thief comes near and no moth destroys. For where your treasure is, there your heart will be also" (Luke 12:33-34).

. . . .

So, to whom should we give our tithe?

The prophet Malachi states that we should bring our tithe into the "storehouse." Although there are various interpretations, I believe the storehouse now refers to one's local church.

As well, there are a number of excellent non-profit organizations in need of our financial support. We see this in the words of Paul and Jesus. Both tell us to use our financial resources to do good and share with those in need. Such offerings are beyond our normal giving to the needs of our church. Both kinds of giving can make an eternal difference in the lives of others.

There's a scene at the end of the movie *Schindler's List* where Oskar Schindler, who started a factory in Poland to save Jews, looked back over the war years, thought of the possessions he still had, and grieved that he had not done more to save others.

Will we feel the same way years from now? Or will we live without regrets?

Summary and Application

Today we've addressed several important concepts about managing our financial resources. We've learned that many Christians have strayed from the teachings of God's Word. Many of us have incorrectly assumed that our worldly possessions are ours. That attitude needs to change as we move toward a proper perspective on God's ownership and our stewardship.

Before we wrap things up today, you may want to spend some time in prayer. You may want to ask God to forgive the ways you've misused your finances and failed to tithe.

We have a lot of work ahead of us this week, but if we can begin to put the truths we learned today into practice, our financial future will be significantly brighter and definitely more blessed by God.

Action Steps for Today

- Confess to God any areas of financial mismanagement.
- Make the commitment to turn over ownership of all your possessions to God.
- Review how you are spending your time and look for ways to establish a more balanced lifestyle.
- Look at your current level of giving and determine what would be an appropriate amount to give on a regular basis.
- Determine what the concept of financial freedom means to you.
- Make the commitment to tithe, starting this week, and continue it for the next six months . . . and hopefully beyond!

changing your
financial status

"Too many people spend money they haven't earned
to buy things they don't want
to impress people they don't like."
—Will Rogers

Based on your work the past two days, and your commitment to keep reading, I'm confident you're someone who desires to make positive and permanent financial changes.

If you agree, congratulations! You are well on your way toward financial freedom.

Today we will explore possible changes you can make to balance your budget, and to create the financial margins that will enable you to save for the important life goals you will identify tomorrow.

The sizes and types of financial changes you will need to make directly relate to your current financial status, which we determined together during Day 1.

If your expenses are grossly out of balance with your income, you will need to make a number of significant changes to balance your accounts.

If you are slightly out of balance, the changes will be fewer and probably smaller. Still, you will need to make enough changes so you can build up your savings and fund some of your longer-range plans and goals.

The completion of today's activities may require some creative thought, some compromises, and a possible lifestyle change or two. If you're married, do all you can to avoid disagreements with your spouse. Instead, keep an open mind as you consider possible options. You both need to put "everything on the table" and be able to talk openly as you brainstorm and weigh potential changes. Remember—everything we own is the Lord's!

PRACTICAL EXAMPLE

Bill and Susan have been married for about 15 years. Due to over-spending by both individuals, they have built up $25,000 in credit card debt, and are currently overspending by $500 per month. Bill is an avid fisherman and will not hear of getting rid of his fishing boat or any of the accessories he has accumulated over the years. Instead, he has directed Susan to stop spending so much for weekly groceries. He is requiring her to reduce grocery expenses by no less than 50 percent, because he is convinced this is where their true problem lies.

The problems in this example are glaring, aren't they? Scenarios like this can cause serious disagreements, frustrations, and undue marital stress. Left unchecked, such financial stressors ultimately can lead to divorce.

One recent study concluded that 90 percent of divorcing couples in the U.S. point to financial disagreements as one of the leading causes of their ruined marriage. Of course, divorce only compounds each person's financial woes. In reality, if a divorce occurs the spending needed to support two households will almost double—adding to the financial stress, not taking it away.

Individuals and couples in financial distress need to work together. Among other things, they need to see if other issues could be adding to their problems.

If any day is going to cause disagreements, it will be today. But it doesn't have to be that way.

If you are single, it may be wise for you to pair up with a good friend who can provide constructive criticism and independent advice as you review your spending patterns.

Carefully and prayerfully get ready for a life-changing day. Whatever you do, don't argue (even with yourself!) and don't stop reading.

. . . .

Determining the Necessary Changes

Day 3 is not about just cutting expenses, but also about increasing our spending in other necessary areas, including giving, savings, and investments. The goal is not only to balance our budget, but also to bring it in line with God's plan for our lives.

Determining which expenses to reduce, or increase, is a process that takes some time and careful reflection. It will also require us to identify what expenses are absolute necessities, and which are nice but not necessary for our survival. The absolutes need to be funded before niceties, preferences, and other discretionary items are even discussed.

In the next section we will begin to identify absolute necessities. Of course, many items that didn't even exist 5 or 10 years ago are often see as today's "absolutes." In reality, if we did not have access to them for a while we would miss them, but we certainly could survive without them!

This past year my cell phone broke. I was told it would be cost-prohibitive to get it repaired since I was due to receive another free phone in two months. So, I went without a cell phone for a few weeks.

Normally, I am a heavy user of cell phones, and for the first few weeks I almost went through a form of withdrawal. After this initial shock wore off, however, I almost appreciated the silence and freedom of being "unavailable" at times. While I did get my brand-new cell phone at the end of two months, I knew it was no longer an absolute. If I wanted to, or if our budget was tight, I could get along just fine without one.

. . . .

Breaking Down Absolute Versus Non-Absolute Expenses

Worksheet 5 in the back of this book will help you identify the financial absolutes and financial non-absolutes in your life.

Before going through this worksheet with your spouse or friend, take the time to fill out the worksheet on your own. This extra step may prevent a painful argument a few minutes from now.

Remember—an absolute expense is one that we must incur each month for our survival. Examples include food, basic transportation, and rent or mortgage payments.

A non-absolute expense is one that funds something we like to have, but it is not critical to our survival. This list includes a number of items we could give up, if needed. Examples include cable television, cell phones, hobbies, and activities.

Take the time now to review your current monthly expenditures to determine whether each is an absolute or non-absolute expense. In some cases, you'll quickly identify items you can eliminate. Then review the other non-absolutes and ask yourself, *Can I live without this, too?*

Resist the temptation, however, to rush out and cancel certain monthly expenses. Instead, simply identify possible cuts. Have some fun...but don't get ahead of yourself!

PRACTICAL EXAMPLE

One of the fast-growing businesses in recent years has been self-storage warehouses. It never ceases to amaze me that people pay more than $75 per month to store $37.50 worth of stuff. While these goods may have been "necessities" at one point, today they're anything but. Getting rid of this clutter and junk may prove to be a very freeing experience. If anything, you can donate the useable stuff to the Salvation Army or Goodwill—and start saving a big chunk of money!

Ideas for Balancing Your Budget

Now that you've finished Worksheet 5, it's time to consider all of the possible options to reduce your monthly expenses. Some non-absolutes can be eliminated with a simple phone call or letter. But be sure to look at additional ways to reduce your expenditures.

Some of the ideas listed below may work for you, while others may not. You certainly don't need to implement all of these ideas, but you do need to identify several ways to increase your savings and give yourself the margin you need to fund your longer-term goals.

. . . .

Telephone, Internet, Television: Find Ways to Trim Costs

Once entailing a relatively small expense, telephone (including cell phones), Internet access, and cable television costs have increased exponentially the past few years. Although most of these expenses were once perceived as discretionary, most people now consider them necessities. Thankfully, there are a number of ways to reduce or eliminate these costs.

If everyone in the family has a cell phone, is there a real need for a home phone, too?

Does everyone in your household (including teenage children) really need to have a cell phone? Or can a limited number of phones be shared among your children?

Also, if you have multiple phones, are you on a family shared plan? Or have you shopped around to make sure you are getting the best rate based on the usage patterns within your family? Of course, watch out for low introductory rates that suddenly jump up in price and leave you locked in for two or more years.

You may want to give your kids prepaid cell phones with a fixed number of minutes.

Many children tend to spend endless hours with calls to friends and hundreds (or even thousands) of text messages. Having phones with limited minutes will cause your children to learn to live within a budget, while still giving you the peace of mind that they'll always have a phone handy in case of emergency.

PRACTICAL EXAMPLE

As our children get older, all of them think they need a cell phone. After all, most high school students have one and, when my daughter was still 12, so did a number of her friends. Although as parents we want to be able to contact our children (and vice versa), the cost of each child having a cell phone is significant. One solution that we use is a pay-as-you-go plan. My high school son, now that he pays the costs, has dropped from about $25 per month as an add-on to our family plan, to only $80 per year as long as he stays within his minutes. We love it because (a) he has a phone and (b) he is learning to wisely budget both his time and money.

Carefully budgeting telephone expenses isn't the only way to save money.

If we need cable television, do we really need all of the premium channels? In our household we made the decision to not subscribe to cable television. Instead, we use an indoor television antenna. With it and the new digital system we can watch fifteen channels at no cost. As an added bonus, we watch fewer hours of television and have found a number of other more productive activities to pursue in our free time.

Those who find it difficult to give up their favorite television shows can do their homework, shop for competitive options, and select the one with the lowest overall cost. Typically, cable services are highly competitive, offer many incentives, and allow you to negotiate cost reductions.

When it comes to Internet service, most individuals, couples, and families can save a lot of money. We certainly don't need the fastest Internet speed available for e-mail. In our family's case, the cost of switching to a lower speed was a painless cut that has saved us hundreds of dollars.

With the convergence of technologies, you may be able to combine products and services to receive discounts from a single provider. If you have home phone service, check about getting cable service from the same provider. If you have cable, check about getting your Internet service from the same company.

Before you finish this section, look at how much you're spending and ask yourself, "Is this is the best way to utilize God's money? What is truly a need?" Although it may be difficult to give up some entertainment and communication options, maybe God wants you to enjoy more time with those you know, love, and cherish.

PRACTICAL EXAMPLE

While a new cell phone may seem quite attractive or have a low initial cost, by the time you add all of the provider charges, monthly service fees, and taxes, the real cost can grow quickly. Also, before you enter into a long-term contract, it is important to discuss all of the benefits and disadvantages, and make sure you have the money to pay for the service throughout the length of the contract.

. . . .

Groceries: Find Ways to Buy on Sale

Groceries are a necessary expenditure. Although food can be a relatively large monthly expense, there are plenty of ways to save money.

First, you can change where you shop. Where we shop can have a significant effect on our expenses. Low-cost food stores have most food staples at a lower cost than fancier grocery store chains.

Second, you can purchase fewer pre-made dinners and make the same meals yourself. In two-income families, where time is often at a premium, purchasing meals at the grocery store's deli may save some time, but the meals costs a lot more.

A fun activity for your family may be to have a "Dinner Making Night." You can all take part making multiple supper entrees that can be frozen and then later popped into the oven or microwave. A benefit for Mom: Your kids will be much more willing to eat what's for dinner!

Third, you can purchase rice and noodles and other basic food staples in bulk.

PRACTICAL EXAMPLE

In a regular grocery store, a bag of un-popped popcorn costs about $1 per pound. At a warehouse store, however, I can purchase 50 pounds of popcorn for $16. While I need to find appropriate storage for this and other bulk items, it does not take long for our family to start saving money.

Fourth, you can use a grocery list when you shop. Grocers are particularly good marketers, and often will offer a plethora of products that they know you will want. And, sure enough, you will buy them if you don't stick to your grocery list. By sticking to your list, you will have a much greater chance of saving money week after week.

Fifth, when you build up a surplus in your grocery budget, use that surplus to purchase staple foods when they go on sale. In our home, we have now built up quite a surplus in our food budget, and often can take significant advantage of sales to purchase the items we use most.

Our family happens to eat an average of one can of corn weekly. So, when the price of corn is marked down to $0.25 per can from its usual price of $0.75 per can, I purchase 52 cans of corn (thereby cutting our annual cost for this item by two-thirds).

PRACTICAL EXAMPLE

Purchasing items on sale is not the only way to save on grocery bills. We often purchase our groceries in bulk (often from warehouse clubs) and split up the quantity among family and friends. By purchasing this way we can purchase the items more often, and all of us can realize the savings.

As well, our family often purchases large quantities of chicken and hamburger when they are on sale. Granted, stores often put limits on the number of items someone can purchase on sale, and they do this because of people like me!

When items go on sale, however, don't go overboard. We will achieve savings only if we are going to use the items, and there's not a risk of them spoiling before we use them.

PRACTICAL EXAMPLE

For me, grocery shopping has become a game. Many grocery stores now list your purchase savings on each receipt. I don't feel as if I have had a successful grocery shopping experience unless the amount I save is more than the amount I spend. I don't do it every time, of course, but I have done it a lot. You can, too.

. . . .

Christmas: Creative Gifts and Giving

The one time of year most people overspend is Christmas. Although we all want to give gifts at Christmas, our biggest tendency year after year is to spend too much. Knowing this, our family has one of two choices at Christmas.

First, we can stay within budget month after month and save the necessary money to purchase the items we want to give.

Second, if we didn't save enough money for lots of Christmas shopping, we either give fewer presents or make our own gifts.

As I look at all of the Christmas presents I've given to my children over the years, they're often played with for only a few days and soon forgotten.

A number of years ago, when my son was much younger, he often had more fun with the cardboard boxes the presents came in than with the presents themselves. Other parents have told me the same thing.

Furthermore, personal gifts created by us for our children may have more lasting value. I know many families do this every year, and I applaud them for doing so. Often it is done out of necessity, but they're blessing their children by their creativity and careful stewardship of the money God has provided. Those twin blessings probably will stay with the children all of their lives.

True, many of us want to give exceptional presents to our children, especially when they are young. But taking on debt to do so negatively affects our children for years to come.

Some critics say that not spending excessively for Christmas presents is un-American, since many firms depend on Christmas spending to carry them through the rest of the year. Still, you must consistently look at what is best for your family long-term, and not worry about how your small family's spending affects the overall economy.

PRACTICAL EXAMPLE

Last year my younger daughter wanted a bed set for her American Girl doll that cost over $100 from the American Girl store. As I looked at the set in the catalog, it looked like just a few pieces of plastic put together with some fabric for the bedspread and canopy. My wife, who is rather creative, stated she could easily make one of these. At Christmas, my daughter received a bed set my wife made that almost matched the one in the American Girl catalog. In fact, our daughter didn't even realize it wasn't the actual set until my wife told her that she had made it. Now my daughter treasures the bed set even more because it's the handiwork of her mom. Total cost for all of the materials to make the bed: $15. Savings: $85.

. . . .

Dining Out on a Budget

Can a family eat out periodically and still rein in their budget? I believe they can if they do the right things.

As everyone knows, the cost of eating out has risen significantly over the years. This is especially true now that my kids are too old to order off the children's menu. Still, I love to eat out and often look forward to trying new restaurants.

Here are a few ways we've found to save money.

First, my kids love to go to fast food hamburger restaurants, and most of them have a special or eat from the dollar menu. I love to watch the face of the clerk when we order ten double cheeseburgers and five chicken sandwiches without fries or drinks. My son, who has a healthy appetite, gets plenty to eat without breaking the bank.

PRACTICAL EXAMPLE

At some McDonalds restaurants, the cost of a single cheeseburger is $.99 while the double is $1.00. I've also seen cases where a single hamburger is more than the double cheeseburger, or 4 chicken nuggets costs $1.00 and six costs $2.79. It's a no-brainer: Order two 4-piece chicken nuggets, throw away the extra two nuggets, and still save $.79.

Purchasing items on the low-cost menu can save you money as long as you don't fill up on all of the higher priced items.

Second, when our family goes out to eat we limit ourselves to certain items. Typically, we do not purchase appetizers or desserts, either of which can cost almost as much as the meals. Instead of spending $20 for desserts, we go somewhere else and order sundaes off a dollar menu.

As well, we do not order drinks in a restaurant. I am not referring to just alcoholic drinks, but also to soda. Purchasing a few glasses of soda can add $10 or $12 to our dining bill. At most restaurants we drink water, which is healthier than soda. We wait until we are home to enjoy two liters of ice-cold soda that cost us $.79 (purchased on sale).

Another strategy we use is coupons and other discount programs. We like to purchase an entertainment book for our area. Similar books are available in major cities across the United States, and part of the proceeds usually benefits a local organization. These entertainment books allow us to try a variety of restaurants at half their normal cost. When we select the restaurant for a particular evening, it is not unusual for us to take out our coupon book and page through it. Another service I have used lately is Restaurant.com. This service allows us to purchase gift certificates at a discounted price. The cost is usually $10 for a $25 restaurant gift certificate. That certificate usually mandates that you purchase $35 of food to use it. When you open an account at Restaurant.com (which is free), you will often receive an e-mail that gives you a code telling you where you can purchase the gift certificates for 50 percent to 80 percent off. Therefore, a $25 gift certificate can cost only $2 to $5 and a $35 restaurant bill will only cost you $12 to $15 total. Talk about a great deal!

By using these discount programs, I find we eat out more often, we usually eat at a higher class restaurant, and we can go out for less than the overall cost of many fast food options.

. . . .

Clothing

Clothing costs have become a significant expense for many Americans. Our children are often being accepted or shunned based on the clothing or labels they are wearing. Although it is important for our children to be accepted, it is also important that we be reasonable in this regard. There are a number of strategies that may help reduce our expenses in this area.

First, shop when things are on sale. Many stores have back-to-school specials, but the better time to purchase such items may be during an after-season closeout. This, however, may be easier for some of us who have older children than for those with growing younger children. Second, shop the garage sales of upper scale subdivisions. Many of these families purchased the name brand products you and your kids want, and are selling them for a small fraction of what they paid for them. This way, you or your kids can have the name brands, and you can stay within your budget.

Third, you can shop at consignment or Goodwill stores. I have talked with a number of people who reported that the best clothing selection of the year takes place the week between Christmas and New Year's, during which good clothing can be picked up for a small fraction of original value. It is during this time that older, but still good, clothing is thrown out to make room for the new clothing received as Christmas presents.

Last, let's all start a trend toward generic. There is usually no difference in quality between a $15 shirt and a $55 logoed shirt other than the potential status it conveys. To stay within our budgets, we need to realize a shirt is a shirt. We should not need to prove a status in life! We should understand that God loves us the way that we are and being pleasing to Him should be the ultimate goal.

. . . .

Making the Necessary Changes

We are now at the point where changes in your spending habits must be made. Although you may feel a little apprehensive about making some of these changes, it is the only way that you can change your financial situation and move toward financial freedom.

In this section you looked at a number of possible ways you could change your budget—not only to balance it, but also to develop surplus funds that can be allocated toward the longer term goals you will be developing later this week.

Worksheet 6 in the back of this book will guide you in deciding which changes to make. This worksheet can be used as a guide to list possible budget reductions and the dollars you would save as a result. This process—though sometimes difficult—is necessary, significant, and worthwhile to you in the longer term. In many cases, though, you'll find this exercise exciting, even exhilarating. Why? Because you'll enjoy the immediate satisfaction of making good, healthy financial choices that will pay substantial long-term dividends.

Remember, you need to eliminate overspending each month, and then cut your expenses even further in order to add margin for unexpected expenses and help accelerate the payoff of your debts.

As you go through this process, don't forget the adage, "You can pay me now or later." If we want everything now (which has been America's motto for a generation), we will have to make substantive sacrifices later—and probably not have enough funds to support us in our later years. By making budget reductions now, you will experience increased contentment in coming months and enjoy many more options later in life, too.

As you go through this process, I pray that the peace of the Lord will come upon you and that a sense of God's peace will be yours to enjoy for months and years to come.

. . . .

Creating a Balanced Budget

Now that you have identified all your necessary budget changes, the time has come to put your new budget into action.

Although this may sound easy, the reality is that following through with these changes, and not reverting back to old ways may be a difficult process for you. It may require significant dedication, some personal sacrifices, and compromises between spouses (if you're married).Worksheet 7 at the back of this book is a record of your previous levels of spending, the effects of the changes you have agreed to make, and your new spending levels.

Again, I want to reiterate that the goal is not just to have a balance between monthly income and expenses. You also want to create a surplus that can offset your debt and increase your savings.

You may want to save Worksheet 7 for years to come so you can document the dramatic positive effects of the changes you're making today. Believe me, it will be fun for you to go back and see the progress you have made. And, if you become discouraged anywhere along the way, you can always go back to this worksheet for encouragement.

Again, be sure to take the actions necessary to make today's changes a permanent reality. Once your monthly income adequately exceeds your expenses, you can go on to the next section of today's work.

. . . .

Keys to Effective Budgeting

To ensure that you stay on track and don't revert back to old patterns of spending, it's time to finalize your household budget.

With the possible exception of Bill Gates or Warren Buffett, everyone needs a budget.

Over the years I have seen many budgeting systems. Some are incredibly simplistic; others are highly complicated. Before we talk about the mechanical aspects of budgeting, we should take time to review what I consider my top seven essential keys for effective budgeting.

Key 1: Find something that works for you and stick with it!

The form your budget takes is not critical as long as it provides you with pertinent information to make effective financial decisions. Regardless of which budgeting system you choose, it will need to be personalized in order to meet your individual requirements.

My particular method of recording my monthly transactions and entering them into my budget may or may not work for you. My system works for me, but it is a result of many years of trial and error. For years now I have used Quicken along with software on my cell phone that interfaces with this system. As I make expenditures, I enter this information into my cell phone, and this information is uploaded to my Quicken software every time I sync the phone with my computer. In addition, all of my credit card transactions are automatically downloaded and matched with the information uploaded from my phone.

Most readers probably will say my system is too "hi-tech" or complex. It works for me. You need to find an effective system, though, that works for *you.*

Often when an individual or couple starts using a system, they run into problems and stop using it. That's the wrong thing to do! If you are using a system that does not work for you, you should identify the specific factors causing problems and change them. Only if that doesn't work should you start looking for another system.

Key 2: Keep Your Budget Simple

Budgeting should not be complicated. Your system should have only enough categories to direct your spending and to track items you'll need to report later when you do your taxes. Furthermore, your system should take no more than 20 to 30 minutes per week. If your current budgeting system takes more than an hour per week, you may want to look for ways to modify and streamline it.

PRACTICAL EXAMPLE

At one of my budgeting seminars, a person presented his intriguing budgeting system. It consisted of a single piece of paper the size of a business card. Each day this individual would write down his income and expenses for the day. He knew that if his income each day was more than his expenses, he would not get into financial trouble. While I do not endorse any one single budgeting system, I believe many of them will work quite well if they are used consistently. Furthermore, regardless of which system you select, you'll need to personalize it based on your particular circumstances and needs.

Key 3: Work on Your Budget Together

It is important that you develop your budget with a partner for two reasons: training and accountability. Doing your budget with someone else creates a valuable form of accountability. If you are a single person, I encourage you to find a good friend who can help you set up your new budget and serve as your accountability partner. If you're married, I trust you're already working with your spouse on each of these exercises. Your spouse's involvement is essential!

Each time I purchase something, I know my wife will be looking at that expenditure at the end of the month with me, and will have something to say if my spending is out of line. Knowing this monthly review will occur works wonders. It almost always helps me stay within budget.

For instance, I like to spend money on books so I have a monthly budget for such purchases. When I see a new book I want to purchase, and then see it costs more than this month's remaining budget allows, I typically wait another month to actually purchase it. Of course, I sometimes forget I really wanted that book by the start of the next month, or I end up borrowing it from a friend or our local library. The key is, I have a budget and I use it. If I don't, I've given my wife permission to gently chide me for spending too much.

My wife doesn't like me to mention this next fact, but—based on my life expectancy—I know I have a good chance of dying before my wife does. I also know that one of my responsibilities as a husband is to make sure that my wife is taken care of, and has the necessary knowledge to make effective financial decisions after I depart this world.

In my case, my wife sometimes would rather go to the dentist than review our budget. Nevertheless, we put forth the effort and take the time to both understand where we are financially and decide how to pay the bills we receive each month. Over time, we've set up most of our bills to be paid electronically, which saves us several dollars on postage each month.

I know I need to make sure there is enough money in our checking account each month to cover these automatic payments. If my spouse does not know this, however, and something were to happen to me, she could quickly run into major problems. It sounds hypothetical, but it happens to new widows and widowers all the time.

PRACTICAL EXAMPLE

One of my clients called to tell me his wife had just died. Unfortunately, his spouse had never taken the time to train him in their finances. He had no idea what to do. While the husband often dies first, there is a chance it may be the wife. Lesson learned: Wives need to train their husbands!

Key 4: Keep Track of All of Your Expenses

Many miss this important concept during the initial stages of the budgeting process. You need to make sure you have a budgeting system that allows you to record everything. Then you need to actually do it!

Often when I meet with individuals to go over their budget, they will assure me they're listing all of their expenses. But when we study the numbers, they often have a large surplus of funds on paper at the end of each month. In reality, though, they are going farther in debt each month. The problem usually is their "**MISC**ellaneous" category, which is another name for **M**oney **I S**pent **C**arelessly. There's no such category in *your* budget, right?

In order to ensure you are accurately recording *all* of your financial transactions *(not just the ones in your checkbook)*, you need to record every penny you spend for the next 30 days. To accurately record these transactions, be sure to use Worksheet 10 in the back of this book.

Recording all of your expenses for a month may sound a bit challenging, but it's the only way you'll know with certainty whether you are staying on track with your budget.

Key 5: Develop a Reasonable Lifestyle

For some, life is meant to be enjoyed, and if it takes money they will use it in order to live life to the fullest. For others, frugality is the rule, saving for the future is what is important, and any enjoyment of life that costs money is out of the question.

So, what *is* a reasonable lifestyle? Well, it's certainly one you can afford.

Although the components of a reasonable lifestyle may vary, we must develop a lifestyle in which we live within our means. It's unreasonable to attempt to enjoy a $120,000 per year lifestyle if you make only $35,000 per year. I often tell my clients, "It's time to act your wage."

In our status-conscious society, however, we often incorrectly believe we are the only ones who don't have something. The availability of easy credit and debt seems like a bridge. Sure, they allow us to enjoy a more expensive lifestyle for a season or two. After a while we almost start believing "we can have it all now." We discover easy credit and debt are trap doors to financial disaster after it's too late.

All of us should enjoy this life, doing so with a consciousness of the calling that God has given to each of us, and doing so at a level commensurate with our current wages.

Two inescapable questions:

- Is your current lifestyle reasonable based on your level of income?
- Are you honoring God with your resources, or are you honoring yourself in a vain attempt to feel more successful?

PRACTICAL EXAMPLE

George and Phyllis Spender currently have $8,000 in credit card debt. If they make the minimum payments at 18 percent, it will take 25 years to pay it off, and they will end up paying $24,000.

Key 6: Know When to Say Enough Is Enough

How often don't we look in our closets and say we don't have a thing to wear—and in our cupboards or refrigerators and say we have nothing to eat—even though both are stuffed to capacity?

What we're really saying is that nothing jumps out at us, we're too lazy to look or cook, or nothing suits our fancy at the moment.

Contentment with what we have currently is a marvelous strength. By exercising this strength, we rid ourselves of untold problems and develop an amazing sense of freedom, joy, and relief.

If we learn to say what we have today is enough, we'll be happier for years to come.

PRACTICAL EXAMPLE

The size of the average American home has grown over the past quarter of a century from under 1,500 square feet to more than 2,000 square feet of living space. Much of this extra space comes from enlarged kitchens and multiple baths. Ironically, we still don't have enough space to hold all of our stuff.

Key 7: Develop an 80/20 Mentality

Most people know and can apply the 80/20 principle. If you are a manager, you know that 80 percent of your problems are caused by 20 percent of your employees. If you are in business or in sales, you know that 80 percent of your revenue comes from 20 percent of your customers.

This 80/20 principle also applies to our finances. It means living on 80 percent of what we make so we can give 10 percent of what we make to God and put the remaining 10 percent in savings.

How much better to live by the 80/20 principle than spend 100 percent or more of what we make every month, creating more burdens than we care to admit!

What budget cuts do you want to make in order to live by this rule?

....

Budgeting Systems

In the previous section we listed a number of keys to consider when we set up our budgeting system. Now we will look at a number of budgeting systems that will allow us to manage our finances effectively. Without these systems, we constantly will wonder where our money went.

The basic systems described in the following pages work effectively for most people. However, we all have different needs and abilities when it comes to managing our finances. If one of these systems works, great! If it doesn't work, we need to remember one of the first keys and identify the parts that are not working for us, then modify the system to address these issues. Developing a system that will meet our overall needs is very important, so we need to continue to make progress with the system we're using and not give up. When I first started preparing a budget for my own family, it quickly became clear I needed to make some adjustments. Our household budgeting system continues to evolve as our lives change. You'll probably need to do the same with your system. Modify your budget system until it's truly *yours.*

In case you don't already have one, here is a brief explanation of the three most common budgeting systems.

Envelope Systems

To set up this type of system you simply take a stack of envelopes and label them with the names of all of the categories you want to track.

When you get paid, you take predetermined amounts of cash and put them into the various envelopes. When you need to pay a bill, you simply go to that respective envelope and take out the money necessary to pay it. If you want to go out for pizza and a movie on Friday night, you simply check your entertainment envelope. If it has only a few dollars left, you make other plans.

Watch out for the temptation to rob from your utilities envelope so you can enjoy a night out, thinking you'll be able to pay the money back later. That's often not the case, and you'll end up short when it comes time to pay your electric bill. What goes in a given envelope stays in that envelope until it's time to pay that particular bill.

If you decide to use this system, create envelopes only for the major budget categories. In the past I have seen individuals with 50, 100, even 150+ envelopes. It's almost impossible to maintain such a system. Keep your envelope system as simple as possible.

The benefits of the envelope system include being simple and easy to use. It also provides you with a level of tangible control over your finances.

The disadvantages of this system can include the failure to create and fund envelopes for savings and longer-range variable expenses.

Modified Envelope Systems

With the modified envelope system you deposit your paycheck into a checking account, and then divide the amount of your check into both normal monthly and variable categories.

Worksheet 8 can assist in further dividing these amounts into various subcategories based on the percentages you determined during the budget process. You then simply deposit the various monthly amounts onto individual account pages (Worksheet 9) and diligently keep track of what you spend (Worksheet 10). Think of each payment as a withdrawal from an individual account page. At the end of each month, remove any remaining balances from your individual account pages and add them to the account savings page (Worksheet 11).

Let's suppose you were going out on Friday. With the modified envelope system, you would simply look at your account page to see what amount you have within this category.

In addition, as you pay your variable expenses, you move funds from your account savings pages to your individual account pages to pay your bills.

When you receive your monthly account statement from your bank, you can use the checking account reconciliation worksheet (Worksheet 12) to make sure the amounts you have in your system balance with the amounts recorded at the bank.

Although this modified envelope system may seem a bit complicated or labor intensive, it shouldn't take much time before you are recording transactions like a pro. Maintaining this system should not require more than an hour per week.

This system has a number of advantages including being fairly simple to use and providing a high level of control (as you record all of your expenses and keep all of your balances readily at hand on individual account pages). For these reasons, it should meet the budgeting needs of most individuals and households today.

Using Technology (Software)

As you continue to develop your budget, you may want to use electronic tools or Web-based systems to help you record your transactions faster and to provide real-time feedback about the balances in each of your accounts. These electronic tools help reduce errors and also can provide feedback concerning the performance of your investment accounts.

With these systems you can generate and print a variety of expense, savings, budget, and investment reports that will help ensure your budget stays on track. In addition, these systems are especially helpful in identifying specific kinds of expenses during tax season.

Most people who opt to use electronic budgeting select Quicken from Intuit Inc. This program is updated annually, and provides a number of electronic links to financial institutions, which can eliminate the need to manually record all of your transactions. As well, there are a number of versions from basic to advanced. Software programs have unique advantages, and are excellent in providing you with the necessary tools to effectively manage your personal finances.

Then again, other options include a new group of Web-based financial programs (including the one listed above). The advantages of an online system include being able to access your information anywhere, being able to link the software to financial institutions for real-time updates, and having all of your financial data backed up on a regular basis.

Still, there are some downsides. Having all of your financial data on a remote system doesn't help if you are in an area that doesn't have high-speed Internet connectivity readily available. As well, there is the potential risk that the hosting company could "data mine" your financial information. So, choose wisely.

If you're just getting started, it may be wise for you to start out with a manual system. Once you get your finances under control, you can then decide whether to move to one of the electronic systems.

. . . .

Making the Commitment to Change

When it comes to personal finances, we all have the ability to make necessary life changes, but often we don't have the corresponding *desire* to change.

The commitment to change today rests with you! Do you have this desire?

The only way you will be able to transform your finances is to have both the desire and commitment to change.

If you are married, both spouses must have this desire and commitment. Of course, God often puts two very different people together in marriage, with differing desires and levels of commitment, and with differing desires for accountability. Remember if you are married that the changes you are making will benefit both of you.

. . . .

Dealing with Failure

It is my hope that you have the desire to make significant changes in your life, that you will implement the necessary changes, and that you will be successful in honoring God with your finances.

Again, everyone has the ability to make positive changes, but it is also very easy for one to fall back into bad habits, especially habits that caused your financial problems in the first place. The Word of God in the book of James states:

> Consider it pure joy, my brothers, whenever you face trials of many kinds, because you know that the testing of your faith develops perseverance. Perseverance must finish its work so that you may be mature and complete, not lacking in anything (James 1:2-4).

Positive change takes time. God is never in a hurry. So, even though you have confessed your sins, and have given control of your finances to God, don't expect God to solve all of your problems immediately. Instead, you may need to live with some of the consequences of past poor decisions for years to come.

Although God may honor your requests and transform your financial picture overnight, it's much more likely that God is working in your life through your finances. Just don't push God out of the way and try to do it all on your own. He will continue to be teaching you life lessons as you continue this journey. In a financial crisis, individuals often confess their sins, look for the miracle cure, and expect that God will transform their finances overnight. Instead, we need to continue to believe that God is always faithful and will provide for all of our needs.

We need to continue to manage our financial resources in a way that honors God. If we slip back into bad habits temporarily, we need to confess our sins, return to the biblical principles of money management, and move forward again. Your current financial condition probably was caused by years of poor financial management, so don't be surprised if it takes a few years to remedy the situation. Don't look for the quick fix. Instead, take a longer-term view of your goal to become financially free.

. . . .

The Bankruptcy Option

There has been a staggering rise in the number of personal bankruptcies in this country. While bankruptcy may be an option for you by law, God's Word offers a very different perspective.

The wicked borrow and do not repay, but the righteous give generously (Psalm 37:21).

Let no debt remain outstanding, except the continuing debt to love one another, for he who loves his fellowman has fulfilled the law (Romans 13:8).

Although bankruptcy is always an option, I believe the responsibility of paying your debts after bankruptcy is required by God. Ironically, state and federal laws governing bankruptcy may present obstacles for you to do so. Paying one former creditor in preference to another may reopen the entire bankruptcy proceedings. So, it is very important that you obtain competent legal counsel to guide you.

Your attorney may recommend that you save all of the funds you owed and pay everything off all at once. You'll also have to decide if you want to pay off your debts with or without interest.

During periods of economic downturn, the pressures of debt—especially business debt—can cause significant concerns. While many people believe business debt is not theirs, they find out quickly that it becomes personal due to the agreements they made with the bank(s). This debt and the problems associated with it can often stress one's family and other relationships.

. . . .

The Importance of Accountability

With any budgeting system, the importance of accountability cannot be overstated. If you are a couple, hold yourselves accountable to each other. If you are a single individual, find another person you trust to hold you accountable. Without this level of account-ability you will not be able to make the necessary changes you have committed to make.

PRACTICAL EXAMPLE

When I was a child I would try to steal cookies from my mother's cookie jar when no one was looking. If I knew I would not get caught, I would be less cautious about taking another cookie. The same is true with our finances, even as adults. If no one is watching, it is much easier to rob from the wrong envelope or from our savings to go out on Friday night. We need accountability both to another human being and to God.

One excellent way you can establish accountability is through a program provided free of charge by Crown Financial Ministries. If you log onto www.crown.org, you can request a volunteer coach in your area. This coach will walk with you throughout the process of making necessary changes in your life, and be the person who holds you accountable in the days and weeks ahead. This is a highly rec-ommended resource!

Summary and Application

Today we began the process of reviewing the changes you need to make in order to be successful in your journey toward financial freedom.

Among other things, we looked at breaking down your spending into absolutes and non-absolutes, and then determining what you could give up not only to have a balanced budget, but also to pay off debt, build up savings, and accomplish longer-term financial goals.

We also discussed the necessity of selecting and using an effective budgeting system. Such systems may seem restrictive, but they also can be freeing. They allow you to know where you are at any point in time, and also help you make sure your money goes toward the things that matter most to you.

Each of the changes you need to make at this point is personal in nature. So, you need equal measures of commitment, desire, and accountability. The latter can be provided by your spouse, a trusted friend, or a Crown Financial Ministries volunteer coach in your area.

Action Steps for Today

- Determine the level of change you need to make to your lifestyle.
- Use Worksheet 5 to determine absolute and non-absolute expenditures within your household.
- Use Worksheet 6 to create a list of possible spending changes and the effects these changes would have on your budget.
- Make the changes necessary to have a balanced household budget.
- Use the personal spending register worksheet (Worksheet 10) to record all of your expenses.
- Review the keys to budgeting to decide who will be responsible for meeting the various requirements of your budgeting system.
- Review the various types of budget systems, and implement one of them.
- Log onto www.crown.org to request a volunteer coach in your area

. . . .

eliminating life's budget busters

Today we will address several key problems that can derail the best of financial plans. Although many things can cause financial problems, a few crucial issues usually cause the greatest difficulties. We'll review each of these potential problem areas and offer practical solutions. These solutions will allow you to continue to progress toward your goal of financial freedom. So, don't skip a single page!

. . . .

The Problems with Debt

Debt seems to be a "normal" part of life today. Everywhere we look we see mountains of debt. The U.S. government borrows immense amounts of money every day. Corporations use debt to leverage their assets in order to create new competitive advantages. Millions of Americans use debt to finance everything from homes to cars, and from vacations to electronics. Every day we acquire more stuff with money we don't even have.

The use of debt and credit cards to purchase many things is a relatively new concept. The older generation used cash to purchase almost everything when they were younger. If they needed a washer or dryer, they saved up to pay for it. If they didn't have the money in savings, they went without until they did. Many cringe at the way most of us use debt today. Yet a majority of Americans believe debt is helpful, even good. But is it?

For one, I believe the availability of debt has caused the prices of goods and services in many parts of this country to rise. Think what a home would cost today if you were able to get only a five-year loan. The average price of homes would have to be a lot lower. Conversely, the availability of loans and other forms of credit has indirectly caused prices to inflate significantly over the past few decades.

Another problem with debt is the limit it can place on your future. This can happen in two ways. First, by spending today, you will not have the funds to spend on important and necessary items in the future. Second, by incurring debt and its related finance charges, the items you purchase will cost more over time than if you paid cash.

I think we can all agree that using credit makes it much easier for us to purchase (1) things we do not need and (2) things we would not purchase if we had to use cash.

The Bible has some important words of wisdom we should heed:

The rich rule over the poor, and the borrower is servant to the lender (Proverbs 22:7).

Even if we believe we can handle the debt load we currently have, we are still slaves to the lenders. If you don't believe this, try missing one or two car payments, or one or two house payments. If you do, you'll be at risk of losing your car or house, no matter how much you've already paid for them.

. . . .

Shop until We Drop?

For many people, the experience of going to the mall to shop is just as much a sport as hunting or fishing is to others. The experience of shopping is just that—an experience. Some people can spend the entire day looking at clothes without making many—or any—purchases. Others don't understand this, and within families and marriages this can cause a lot of frustration and outright conflict.

I like to joke that some men shop the same way they hunt. They go into one store, find their size quickly, purchase the item, and are out of the store within minutes. I can walk throughout an entire mall, return to the same store where I left my wife, and often find her just a few feet from where she was standing before. How does she do that? It's beyond me.

Honestly, most of us already have too much stuff. Why do so many people need to rent outside storage in the first place? Often it is because they have purchased so much new "stuff" they can't fit it all into their already oversized, overstuffed homes. Why don't we just spend less, consume less, and be more content with what we have already?

If you're married, you and your spouse need to discuss who typically spends more. In the average family, the husband typically spends more than the wife. Women tend to shop more often, but spend smaller amounts on a number of things. Men usually shop less frequently but purchase much more expensive items such as electronics, campers, boats, and sporting equipment. Then again, it can easily be the woman who has difficultly controlling her spending.

Regardless, one of you probably has a problem with spending. Don't be judgmental as God often puts opposites together in marriage to balance each other. Once you identify who it is, you can review his or her spending patterns to determine the extent of the problem and how it usually occurs. For example, if the person typically overspends in particular stores, a simple answer may be to stay away from those stores.

PRACTICAL EXAMPLE

In our family, I often spend a lot of money on books. I know if I go into a bookstore, I will likely come out with a new book that I probably will not have time to read. If I stay out of bookstores, however, I probably won't purchase any new books. Similarly, there is a certain clothing store that causes problems for my wife. Choosing where we do—and don't—shop helps both of us stay within budget.

Much of our economy is built on continued personal consumption and ever increasing levels of spending. However, if we continue to do what we have done in the past, we are going to continue to get the results we got in the past. Unless we choose to make changes, we are only going to get ourselves deeper and deeper into debt.

If you want to change your financial future, you must begin to eradicate some of your past behaviors. Thankfully, when you begin to do things differently you begin to experience significant benefits. One benefit is the satisfaction of knowing, *I'm making the right choice again.* It feels good! So, be sure to follow through on the financial choices you're making this week.

. . . .

Credit Cards

People who use credit cards regularly spend 30 percent more using those cards than if they paid with cash. Retailers know this, which is why more of them not only allow you to use credit cards, but encourage you to do so. Besides, it always seems easier and more convenient to pull out your plastic and use it.

So, are credit cards all bad? No.

One of the ways credit cards can be used effectively is to use them for budgeted expenses only. That way, it's always a planned purchase that you already know is in the budget.

Another way is to take out your checkbook each time you use your credit card and subtract the amount of the transaction from your checking account. Then when you receive the credit card bill, you'll already have the money needed to pay it all off. Of course, this will work only if you make sure you write down every credit card transaction in your check book.

A simpler approach is to use a debit card instead of a credit card, which will remove the money from your checking account when each transaction happens.

There are times credit cards speed up the process or provide other benefits. Just try renting a car without a credit card, or making a hotel reservation in a distant city. In addition, if you travel overseas, you'll find that using a credit card for purchases or cash advances from foreign ATM machines often provides some of the best exchange rates.

In today's increasingly complex financial environment, banks are finding it easier to add additional fees and charges, including late fees and over the limit fees and are even resorting to changing the date or time that a payment is due to cause a payment to be late. I even find it amusing what a bank calls a person who is a responsible spender who pays off his or her card balances each month a "deadbeat"!

In one case, a card company issued multiple low credit limit cards to individuals and then began charging them multiple times for late fees and over-limit fees on top of exorbitantly high interest rates. In one case, the individual had to pay more than $400 in over-limit fees alone.

Credit cards often seem like easy money. Credit cards appear to provide funds to do the things you cannot afford or get things you want to purchase but can't afford yet. But of course, that's an illusion. Promise yourself that you'll never spend money you don't have.

PRACTICAL EXAMPLE

Wally and Sarah Smith have decided to take their children on a family vacation. They use their credit cards throughout the vacation and when they return, discover, they've spent $2,400.00. They have allotted $50 per month in their budget for vacations and travel. They had hoped to take another vacation in two years, but if they pay $50.00 a month at 18 percent interest, it will take them almost seven years to pay off this first trip.

PRACTICAL EXAMPLE

Sam and Mary Builder need a new roof for their home. They knew that the home would eventually need a new roof, but they did not save over time for this cost. The cost of the roof is $4,500, paid with credit cards. At $70 per month, it will take the Builders 16 years to pay off that necessary but costly expenditure. By the time they finally pay it off, it may be time for Sam and Mary to hire someone to replace their roof again. Paying $70 per month for 16 years would actually amount to a total expense of $13,440 for a $4,500 roof.

Again, using credit cards wisely can offer a number of benefits. You can earn miles or points that can be used for airline travel, hotel stays, and merchandise. These are benefits, though, *only if* you use the cards for budgeted items, pay off the entire balance each month, *and* the card doesn't charge interest as long as you don't carry any balance into a second month.

If you ever maintain a credit card balance, or fail to pay your bill on time, the interest and fees you'll end up paying will far outweigh the benefits of any mileage points you might receive.

For many years now, leading financial authors have been writing about the evils of credit cards. Though using credit cards involves many dangers, credit cards are not the real problem. The real problem always is an unwise user.

I am often asked if it is wise to take advantage of the many credit cards that offer cheap interest rates, or to use cards that use substantial interest rate reductions as introductory offers. Yes, I believe these offers can be used to reduce our interest and allow us to pay off our credit debt at a faster rate. One needs to be careful, however, of the interest rate charged after the introductory period. Never fall into the trap of continuing to use the card at the higher rate.

Although it may look good for you to be able to pay off your MasterCard with your Visa, in the long run you need to pay off *all* credit card debt. You'll be so glad you did.

. . . .

Buying Too Much House

The problem for many is not purchasing a house that has too much square footage, but buying one that is too expensive in relation to their income. A generation ago, many families lived in a home with one bathroom for five kids and a one-stall garage for the family car. Today, a bathroom for every person almost seems like a "must," and a three-stall garage seems to be a necessity.

Home ownership with its associated taxes and maintenance costs is expensive. Sadly, many families do not consider the total cost of home ownership before making this lifestyle decision. In addition, problems arise when we want to purchase a home in a desirable neighborhood and it stretches a family's budget to the point where both husband and wife need to work. But the facts on the ground remain the same.

Time is one of the most precious commodities we have, and our kids grow up so quickly. Wouldn't it be better to have a smaller house so we can have a bigger allotment of time together as a family?

Of course, family time isn't the only thing that can be lost. John and Rebekah don't have any children yet, but their situation, to follow, is more common than you might imagine.

PRACTICAL EXAMPLE

John Smith purchased a home in a rather prestigious subdivision. Unfortunately, paying the monthly payments was difficult for him and he could not afford to even furnish much of the home. Both John and his wife, Rebekah, were working two jobs so they could keep the home of their dreams. They noticed that many couples in their subdivision were divorcing, and some whose homes were going into foreclosure. These couples were obviously facing similar financial struggles.

· ·

The Refinancing Trap

Decreases in interest rates often fuel significant increases in the number of home refinances. The lowering of interest rates is a significant benefit to the budgets of many and allows them to reduce their home payments. That's great. What's not great is how many people add to the amount of their loan so they can purchase more "stuff" with the additional funds.

When I refinanced my home recently, I was given the opportunity to borrow an additional $10,000, which I declined to do. However, when I received the loan check, it included this additional $10,000. I believe most people would have simply taken this money and purchased a new fishing boat or taken a "needed" vacation. The more prudent thing to do, however, would be to take this amount and pay it right back on the principle of the loan.

When interest rates are lower, we can normally purchase a larger home at a smaller monthly payment than when interest rates are higher.

Over the past few years, many households have refinanced their home a number of times to take advantage of these lower interest rates.

Some individuals locked into a 30-year fixed rate, but many others opted for adjustable rate mortgages (ARM), which offer a lower interest rate and lower monthly payment. Sadly, most were caught off guard when interest rates rose and their monthly payments rose significantly, too. Such drastic cost increases resulted in millions of loan defaults, especially in sub-prime markets.

It's absolutely critical that we make wise choices when it comes to purchasing a home. Each choice could end up wasting or saving literally tens of thousands of dollars.

PRACTICAL EXAMPLE

Simon and Sharon Banks purchased their $175,000 home 10 years ago on a 30-year mortgage at a fixed interest rate of 10 percent. At this rate their monthly payment was $1,523.06 and, the cost of their home after 30 years would be $548,301 ($1,523.06 times 12 payments per year times 30 years). After 10 years of payments, they determined they still owed $127,792.54. Due to the changing economic environment, they have the opportunity to refinance and set up a new 30-year loan at 6 percent. This would reduce their monthly payments to $762.37 per month, which is a savings of $760.69 per month. Although they could use this savings to enhance their lifestyle in other areas, if they continued to make the larger monthly payments already factored into their budget, they could completely pay off their house in 9 years and save more than $191,000 in interest costs.

Buying Instead of Renting

It's the American dream to purchase a home, and many individuals want to build equity instead of pouring rental payments "down the drain." Even though current interest rates are relatively low, one must carefully consider whether it is wise to purchase a home in this economic environment.

Before you move from renting to purchasing a home, or before you purchase a larger or second home, you need to consider a number of factors. These include your current age and life stage, your current financial position, and the location of the home.

If you are younger, it may be wise to rent until you know exactly where you will be settling down. Many who have taken advantage of low interest rates to purchase a newer or larger home have found it difficult to sell their old house. Also, various parts of the country continue to experience economic difficulties, and selling homes in these areas has become a very difficult and costly experience.

PRACTICAL EXAMPLE

Jamie Smith, age 21, is a recent college graduate paying $650 per month for an apartment. Based on current interest rate levels, she thinks she could afford a home for the same monthly payment. She currently has a few job prospects and a boyfriend in another city. Still, she is strongly considering purchasing a home. But wisdom says Jamie would be better off renting for at least two or three more years until she is sure of where she will end up with a job and where she plans to settle down.

Is It Location, Location, Location?

One of the major factors of home selection is location. Location is important for a number of reasons including the quality of education for your children, the convenience in getting to places such as school and church, and (most importantly) your ability to sell the home in the future at a profit.

To sell your home at a profit, you need to look at what will constitute a good location in the future. Although some communities have an excellent future because of current global trends, other communities are near economically challenged areas, which would hamper your ability to sell your house—let alone sell it for a profit.

Among other things, you need to study population movement and growth trends. As the Baby Boomer population ages, more people are moving toward southern and coastal regions. Currently, two-thirds of the United States population lives within 100 miles of the Atlantic Ocean, the Pacific Ocean, or the southern border of the United States.

Over the next few years, it may be much wiser to purchase a home in a population growth zone rather than regions within the "Rust Belt," which already have suffered significant economic damage and decline.

. . . .

Autos

The love of the automobile has long been associated with the American dream. The automobile, once a means of getting from one place to another, has now become a symbol of status or affluence. Of course, as autos become pricier, the monthly payments on them also have increased significantly.

In addition, we live in an environment in which many families cannot operate with only one car. Most people live in areas with minimally adequate public transportation systems. Beyond that, most family members who are able to drive now "require" a car for their sense of independence.

This section will expand on the various components of this budget buster and give you some concrete suggestions on how to move from financial bondage to contentment and success.

Choosing the Auto that Best Meets Your Needs

When you select a car that best suits your needs, remember today's cars last longer than in the past. So, be sure to keep your future needs in mind. As well, be sure to review the total costs of ownership. Your goal should be to lease or purchase the car that provides the largest return per thousand dollars. Make sure you fully factor in the costs of maintenance and insurance.

As you look at all the great automobiles available today, keep in mind that the basic purpose of an auto is to get you from point A to point B. God gave us two feet to do precisely that, and anything beyond our feet is simply a matter of speed and convenience. However, most Americans focus more on style and status than the basic principle that cars transport us from A to B.

Recently someone told me about a friend who drives a jet black BMW 750i with the vanity license plate "WAS HIS." The woman received it as part of their divorce settlement. Considering the cost of this vehicle, I think a more apt license plate would read "THE BNKS."

Honestly ask yourself three questions:

"Am I using cars to make myself feel more important or to make others feel jealous?"

"Do I believe that the more expensive the car I drive, the more successful I must be?"

"Is this the best use of my limited financial resources?"

Performing Appropriate Maintenance

The cars and trucks produced today are built better than ever, which means they can last many years longer than previous models—if you take the time to maintain them properly. If you follow your car's recommended maintenance schedule, you will usually avoid costly problems later. One of the simplest and least expensive requirements is regular oil changes. But make sure you know what else your car needs—and when.

Should You Purchase New or Used?

I have often heard people say that when you purchase a used car, you're purchasing someone else's problems. Years ago I would have agreed with this, but not anymore.

As previously noted, cars generally last much longer than they did in the past.

As well, large numbers of cars are leased on three-year contracts, which create many excellent opportunities for individuals to purchase used cars with relatively low mileage.

In addition, so much of the depreciation of the vehicle's value occurs within the first few months. Several thousand dollars of resale value can be lost simply driving a new car off the lot. For some, the experience of being able to drive a new vehicle, with all the associated "new car smells," is something they value and can afford. Still, aren't there better ways to invest your money?

Because most auto depreciation occurs within the first 30 months, it is often best to purchase a vehicle that's between two and a half and four years old. Knowing that you purchased a vehicle with the lowest cost versus benefit ratio is a wise choice every time.

Another benefit of purchasing a used vehicle is that it allows you to own a car that's normally out of your price range. It's the best of both worlds. You have the opportunity to drive the make and model you want at a price you can afford.

For example, if you want to drive a Lexus or BMW, purchasing one that is a few years old can shave off half of the cost or more, which could put the car into a price range you can afford.

The Leasing Trap

Leasing has become a more popular option in recent years. However, there are a number of pros and cons to consider before entering into a lease agreement.

In general, leasing has allowed the American consumer to purchase a more expensive car than he or she could afford if it had been purchased for cash or with a loan.

As well, leasing has allowed auto manufacturers to increase their profits by adding many expensive options, which considerably increase the overall price of the car. These price increases are not generally noticed by the average consumer as he or she is usually concerned only about the monthly cost.

Many people argue that they will have to make car payments whether they purchase the car or lease it, so what's the problem with leasing? But is a monthly car payment always necessary? This mindset has contributed greatly to the financially stressed situation many are in today. Having a never-ending monthly auto payment is not a recommended way of using our financial resources in a God-honoring way.

A few years ago, I took the plunge and leased a very nice new car. I leased this vehicle because the company at which I was employed gave me a monthly car allowance. It was expected that, in my position, this car would be traded in every three years.

When I leased this car, I looked at two vehicles. The calculated residual value of one of the cars was higher than the other. Even though the purchase price was higher, the monthly lease payment for this car was lower.

Due to the high mileage I was driving each year, I purchased a lease with a much higher amount of allowable mileage. This higher mileage almost doubled my monthly payments, but saved me a considerable amount at the end of the lease. I was allowed 60,000 miles during the three-year lease period, and when I turned the vehicle in it had 60,043 miles on it, so I ended up paying only $4.30 in extra fees. Often these additional mileage fees are not anticipated, and can cause hundreds or thousands of dollars of extra expenses at the end of the lease.

When I turned in my leased vehicle, I wondered if I should purchase the vehicle for the residual value of the lease. The dealer mentioned, however, that there were other cars on the lot selling for three thousand less than my residual value. In effect, by me leasing this vehicle, it saved me three thousand dollars.

Based on my own experience, I have identified three important factors to consider before entering into a lease agreement. First, find a vehicle with the best lease cost, not the lowest purchase price. Second, purchase a plan with a high enough allowable mileage to meet your driving needs. Third, select a vehicle that has a higher residual value than a comparable model at the expiration date of the lease.

Looked at this way, is leasing all that bad? It depends on the goals of the purchaser. If your employer requires you to change vehicles frequently, leasing may be an excellent option. Among other things, you may avoid potential problems when the resale value of the car is less than the residual value at the end of the lease. Leasing also entails fixed monthly payments over the term of the lease, which may be better if you are a small business owner. In addition, leasing may be preferable if you don't put very many miles on your vehicle each year, since many current leases allow 12,000 or fewer miles each year.

Most people do not need to trade in their vehicles as frequently as manufacturers wish, so purchasing a vehicle and keeping it for a longer period of time typically yields much greater financial benefits. If you can pay for a vehicle within four or five years, the cost of using the vehicle for five or six more years often is minimal, even if you have an occasional maintenance problem.

The bottom line: The best vehicle for you to drive may be the one you already have, especially if you already own it.

Purchasing Your Next Vehicle for Cash

How would you like to purchase your next vehicle for cash? Let me give you a workable strategy to do what many consider "impossible."

Let's assume we can purchase a new SUV for $25,000, and after five years the resale value would be $7,000. Purchasing the SUV over five years at 10 percent interest rate would give us monthly payments of $488.68. Over five years our total payments would be $29,321 ($488.68 x 60 months). If we subtract the resale value of $7,000, the cost of the SUV itself (not counting gas, insurance, and maintenance costs) would be $22,321.

If we purchase a $10,000 used car, however, our monthly payments would be only $169.97. If we made the same payments we would have made on the SUV, we could pay off this used vehicle in 18 months. During the remaining three and a half years we could put the same monthly payments into an investment that yields the same rate of return as the interest we were paying, and have $24,703 in our investment account at the end of five years.

Admittedly, the cheaper used car would not be seen as an indicator of your success, nor would it be highly impressive in your church parking lot. It would, however, be far more attractive financially.

First, the cost of the SUV versus the cheaper car is actually $47,024 ($22,321 outflow versus inflow of $24,703).

Second, by not buying the SUV now, you'll be able to purchase it five years from now for cash!

Can you imagine how great it would feel to be able to walk into a dealership and pay for your next vehicle in cash? However, if you do this, don't be surprised, as I once was, when the salesperson could only quote the monthly cost, and not the outright purchase price.

Being able to pay for a vehicle with cash will surprise everyone. It also may give you some additional leverage as you negotiate the actual sale price.

. . . .

The Lottery / Gambling Trap

In the U.S., more money is now spent on gambling than groceries. It's a sad commentary of the true state of our country, isn't it?

Most lottery advertising focuses on promoting the benefits to either schools or winners. For some reason, they never show the tens of millions of losers. So, more Americans are falling into the lottery trap every week.

Of course, no financial advisor in his or her right mind would endorse gambling. So, what's the faulty thinking behind playing the lottery and other forms of gambling?

First, people believe that because someone is going to win big, that someone could be them (as long as they continue to play). Fact: You have a better chance of being struck by lightning then winning the lottery.

Second, people believe that if they win big, they'll stop gambling and live it up. Fact: People who win small amounts become addicted to gambling and can't stop. According to experts in Las Vegas, if you keep playing, the house eventually always wins.

Third, people believe they can afford to gamble. Fact: Most people waste a large chuck of the money they could have used to retire at age sixty-five.

Fourth, people believe they'll be rich once they win big. Fact: Research studies have proved most winners are bankrupt within a few short years of winning millions because these individuals have already proven that they are not able to handle money.

So far, I have met three major lottery winners. Two were almost completely broke within four years of winning. The third person managed to do well by getting appropriate legal and investment advice and investing the funds appropriately.

Many individuals could become millionaires by investing their funds instead of gambling them away over fifteen, twenty, or thirty years.

PRACTICAL EXAMPLE

If a person stopped gambling and invested $60 a week for 35 years (at a 10 percent return), he or she would end up with a million dollars. If the same person invested $120 a week, they would have a million dollars in 20 years. If he or she invested $240 a week, they would be millionaires in only 15 years. Imagine!

Generally, people who play the lottery most often typically live within the lower levels of our economic system. Regardless of one's economic status, the lottery is a voluntary tax. Why pay it?

Again, society and advertising downplay the facts and wrongly claim we all can be winners! Sadly, there need to be tens of millions of losers for the system to work.

To be good stewards, you and I need to treat our financial resources differently from the rest of the world. Being a winner or loser is not a matter of chance, but a matter of hard work, wise choices, and dedication over time.

America is still the land of opportunity. Interestingly, new immigrants to this country have twice as high rates of entrepreneurial success as those who have lived here for years or all of their lives. Let's never forget there are wonderful opportunities for advancement in this country, regardless of who you are.

We live in a great country, we should be grateful to God for the opportunities we enjoy, and we need to make sure we don't let gambling and other poor choices wreak havoc in our lives.

. . . .

Co-signing for Someone Else

Before we wrap up this chapter, I want to take a few minutes to address what appears to be the most innocuous or improbable budget buster: co-signing someone else's loan. Co-signing means you are agreeing to pay someone else's loan the minute they stop doing so.

A number of passages in the Bible warn against co-signing. Heed these clear-cut warnings:

Do not be a man who strikes hands in pledge or puts up security for debts; if you lack the means to pay, your very bed will be snatched from under you (Proverbs 22:26-27).

A man lacking in judgment strikes hands in pledge and puts up security for his neighbor (Proverbs 17:18).

My son, if you have put up security for your neighbor, if you have struck hands in pledge for another, if you have been trapped by what you said, ensnared by the words of your mouth, then do this, my son, to free yourself, since you have fallen into your neighbor's hands: Go and humble yourself; press your plea with your neighbor! Allow no sleep to your eyes, no slumber to your eyelids. Free yourself, like a gazelle from the hand of the hunter, like a bird from the snare of the fowler (Proverbs 6:1-5).

The Bible couldn't be clearer about this. If you've already co-signed a loan, don't go to bed tonight until you get out from under this trap.

Remember, banks and other companies that loan money are experts. If they have looked at all the evidence and determined that the individual or couple is a substantial credit risk, with a high probability of defaulting on the loan within a year or two (while still enjoying the goods or services rendered), who are we to question their judgment?

Ask anyone in the world of lending. A large majority of the individuals and couples who co-sign loans end up paying those same loans. And their reward? Lost money. Guilt. Shame. Anger. Bitterness.

True, there may come a time when you feel it's necessary to co-sign a loan for a young adult child or extended family member. But don't forget that countless family relationships have been destroyed, and marriages dissolved, over this issue.

In such situations, (1) know in detail what you are guaranteeing to pay, (2) put all of that money in a savings account, and (3) treat the money as a future gift to that family member. It's highly probable you'll have to pay for the loan, so (4) don't act surprised, shocked, or disappointed when that becomes a reality.

Better yet, agree with Scripture's injunctions and never co-sign a loan for anyone, even a loved one or close friend. Instead, in love and wisdom simply say, "I'm sorry, but I can't."

Summary and Application

Today we've discussed some major budget busters. The specific areas are extensive debt, excessive shopping, keeping balances on credit cards, the purchase or refinance of too much home, the purchase of expensive automobiles, playing the lottery and other forms of gambling, and co-signing someone else's loan.

Although any of these can be a budget buster, the combination of several of these almost always guarantees impending financial disaster. We cannot predict the future, but we can begin to prepare for it. So, do whatever you can to escape from each and every one of them.

Action Steps for Today

- Make the commitment to review your lifestyle and deal with any budget busters in your life.
- If you have trouble limiting your credit card spending, cut up your cards and use cash only.
- If you have problems with excessive shopping, make a public commitment to stay away from certain malls or stores.
- If you have problems with your house payments, determine what changes need to be made now and what you need to do differently in the future.
- If you have problems with how much you're spending on car(s), determine what you need to do now and what your requirements will be for your next vehicle purchase (or lease).
- If you buy lottery tickets and spend money on other forms of gambling, stop. Instead, invest that same amount of money every month. Over time, you'll accumulate a great deal of wealth.
- If you have co-signed a loan, get on the phone immediately and get out from under this obligation before you go to sleep tonight.

DAY 5

. . . .

setting goals

Today's activities will move us from many of the numerical elements of our finances to the process of setting life goals. Setting life goals will help you determine both how your funds need to be invested and the resources you'll need to achieve these goals.

Each New Year, millions of Americans make resolutions to lose weight, become more physically fit, or to spend less money. While some of these individuals succeed in their goals, the majority of others do not last past the first week. Why is this? Why can't we achieve the goals that we set for ourselves?

I believe that one of the main reasons for this is that we have no compelling reason to do so. Achieving these goals would be of no specific benefit to us—either materially or personally. Goals should be used to move us from the person we are to the person we are striving to be. Yet, without taking the time to determine what type of person we would like to become, we will find that setting goals will just be a task list to be resurrected again next year.

When developing our goals, we need to take a serious look at who we are, and what we want to become in order to fulfill our purposes here on earth. Such goals instill passion and motivate us to actually accomplish them.

In today's work you will be developing and prioritizing your goals, and then looking to see, based on your projected resources, which ones you will be able to accomplish. As you develop your high priority goals, it will be important to spell out in detail the steps you need to take to attain your goals. Worksheet 14 will guide you through this process.

Most of you will have more goals than you have the resources to accomplish. Does that mean you should remove certain goals from your list? Definitely not! As you move through life some of your goals may change, and you may gain additional resources that could fund either these new or existing goals.

. . . .

Setting Both Short- and Long-Term Goals

As you begin developing your goals, think in both the short and long term. Although society continually pushes us toward short-term thinking, we must continually be aware of the longer-term needs that require our financial resources.

I recently saw an advertisement for a car that I would like to have. When I became aware of the monthly cost of leasing this vehicle, my first response was that I could afford it. Although I could afford it, if

I purchased this vehicle, I would be thinking in the short-term only. By purchasing the vehicle today, I may not have the financial resources that I might need to fund longer term goals for myself and my family.

TRANSFORMATIONAL TIP

We cannot continue to spend for today, and not consider the future.

How do we prevent short term thinking? By defining both short- and long-term life goals! Take the time to do this. It will make a significant difference in your future!

· ·

Defining Your Goals

If you were just diagnosed with a terminal illness and were given only one year to live, how would you want to live out that year? What experiences would you like to have, and how would you treat your relationships with others? Since most of us do not know the number of days in our future, should we not live every day like it is our last?

Develop a list of the things you want to achieve during your lifetime. You can go to the Word of God for advice. Proverbs states:

To man belong the plans of the heart, but from the LORD comes the reply of the tongue (Proverbs 16:1).

Commit to the LORD whatever you do, and your plans will succeed (Proverbs 16:3).

In his heart a man plans his course, but the LORD determines his steps (Proverbs 16:9).

Many are the plans in a man's heart, but it is the LORD's purpose that prevails (Proverbs 19:21).

As seen in the passages cited, we can develop our own ideas and plans, but they will come to fruition only if they are the will of God. Constantly seek and consider God's will as you develop your short and long term goals.

At this point in your journey you need to develop a complete list of all the goals that you would like to achieve from now until the time you die. These goals include specific aspirations for your family, educational ideals, travel plans, significant acquisitions you'd like to make, etc.

I highly encourage you and your spouse to take some time, maybe even to get away for a period of time, to jointly develop your household goals. If you are single, you may want to work with a friend or accountability partner. In the back of this book, Worksheet 13 will help you in listing and categorizing all of these goals.

It is important to make these goals as specific as possible. For example, here are two goals:

- I would like to be debt-free.
- I will be debt-free by December 31, 2012.

Which goal inspires you more? The first goal doesn't have a specific deadline or any assurance that you will successfully complete it. Sure, I "would like" to have a number of good things, but unless I create a quantifiable, achievable goal ("I will") and set a time frame within which to reach it, there is very little chance I will succeed.

In addition, as you develop your goals, it is important to remember that, at this stage in the process, no goal is out of the question or impossible to achieve. Use the worksheet to keep listing goals until you feel you have developed a comprehensive list. I would not be surprised that as you start listing your goals in each of these areas, you may develop a list of 100, 200, or more possible goals you'd like to achieve over the remainder your life.

. . . .

Categories of Goals

It is God's desire for each of us to maintain a balanced lifestyle. As you begin to develop your personal and household goals, it is important to begin to categorize them to ensure that they support this balanced life. In this book, we will define goals in six specific areas: spiritual, family, financial, professional or career, personal, and physical goals.

Don't view each goal as just another task to check off a list. Rather, allow these goals to inspire you to consider who you want to become as a person. Keep all areas of your life in mind. We've all heard accounts of business leaders who put everything into their work only to experience negative (and often disastrous) consequences with their spouse and children. Focusing on only one area, such as a career, will only cause you to become frustrated and experience difficulties in the other areas of your life.

. . . .

Spiritual Goals

Victor Frankl once said that "man's search for meaning is the chief motivation of his life." What part of your life is consumed with seeking meaning and spiritual maturity? God's Word is very clear about the importance of this.

Set your mind on things above, not on earthly things
(Colossians 3:2).

Choose my instruction instead of silver, knowledge rather than
choice gold, for wisdom is more precious than rubies, and nothing you desire can compare with her (Proverbs 8:10-11).

As Christians, we all understand the importance of spiritual
goals in our lives. However, the realities of our day-to-day lives often
come in direct conflict with moving toward these spiritual goals.

I firmly believe that one of the main reasons why we don't read
our Bible more frequently is that our Bibles don't ring, buzz, or text
message. For some, personal time with God has become a daily spiritual priority; they would not trade this time for any earthly activity.
For others, personal time with God has never been a high priority, or
other demands crowd out time devoted to seeking God.

Rather than feel guilty about what we have or have not done, we
need to move forward and develop significant goals in this area.

For those who can't imagine where this time will come from,
it is important to remember that our time on earth is very limited
compared to eternity.

If you are having trouble devoting time to this activity, it may
help you to join a local Bible study group, or seek out an accountability partner whom you can work with. You can begin with something as simple as posting passages of Scripture on your mirrors so
you can memorize important passages. You could also purchase the
Bible on CD or download it on your iPod and listen as you com-
mute to work or jog.

Developing spiritual goals, and spending time in devotions and
Bible study, will result in significant benefits and improved relationships in the other areas of our life.

For the LORD gives wisdom, and from his mouth come knowledge and understanding (Proverbs 2:6).

Whoever has will be given more; whoever does not have, even what he has will be taken from him (Mark 4:25).

So, what are your spiritual goals? Take some time to make a list of 10-20 goals. Spend some time in personal prayer. Seek out God's calling for your life. Dream about how God could use you for His Kingdom. Ask the Holy Spirit to shine light on the areas in your life where He wants you to grow and change.

Today God may be calling on you to do something significant in this area. Listen carefully for God's voice!

. . . .

Family

According to Patrick Morley, author of *Man in the Mirror*, no amount of success we may experience at work will ever compensate for failure at home. One of our primary responsibilities is to others within our family: as a husband, a wife, a parent. As Luke states:

The Lord answered, "Who then is the faithful and wise manager, whom the master puts in charge of his servants to give them their food allowance at the proper time?" (Luke 12:42).

All family members bear responsibilities to each other. A wife is truly a precious gift from God (Proverbs 18:22); God calls a husband to love her in the same way that Christ loves his church (Ephesians 5:25-33). Husbands, take the time to determine your wife's needs and make her a priority in your life. Wives, understand your husband's needs and nourish your relationship with him (Titus 2:4-5).

A great many people today cite financial reasons for failing relationships. I believe, however, that financial problems are just one of the surface issues and often other relationship issues are at stake. More often than not, financial problems are just a cover-up for problems in other areas.

Although financial issues are an important part of family life, taking the necessary time to cultivate relationships is also vital. If you were to look back 25 years from now, what would determine whether you were a successful spouse? With your spouse, create goals that reflect what it will take to ensure that success.

I am reminded that children spell love T-I-M-E! Time spent with our children is a responsibility—and a valuable investment. The pressures of the world often reduce time spent with our children to a minimum. Many parents today work such long hours that they don't have sufficient time to spend with their children. I often wonder why we needed to move from a one-parent income to a two-parent income in less than one generation. In many families both spouses are pursuing their individual career goals, but it is often the case that both are working just to purchase more "toys" or the "stuff" to appear more successful.

Children have become of secondary importance at a time when it is more critical than ever for parents to prepare their children for life and to raise them up as children of God. I often see parents spend hours with their kids on sports, and their children are able to recite many statistics of various sports teams and players. Are you spending the same amount of time with them in developing their spiritual maturity? As well, encourage your children and appreciate their achievements regardless of how small they are; pray for them, and love them unconditionally regardless of what they do.

For many of you, the realities of divorce or the guilt of not raising your children properly may be weighing quite heavily on your heart. You cannot change what has happened in the past, but you are not dead, either. Through God's working and grace, He has given you more time to work with your relationships and bring about peace and possible reconciliation.

As you review your family relationships, you may want to set specific goals for spending the time to make family relationships one of your highest priorities. I firmly believe that positive results will follow! As you list the goals that will strengthen your family life, list also what those accomplished goals will do for you if achieved.

As you later take the time to prioritize your goals, I would hope that many of the ones that you listed under this category will move to higher levels of importance in your life.

Financial

Of course, setting financial goals is essential. Some of the financial goals that you may want to consider are to reduce or eliminate your debt, to increase your personal savings, to save for a child's education, or to save for retirement. Although these may be included with your other personal goals, including these goals under this category will allow you to focus your financial resources on achieving them. The Bible gives excellent advice concerning this:

Trust in the LORD with all your heart and lean not on your own understanding; in all your ways acknowledge him, and he will make your paths straight (Proverbs 3:5-6).

Although we do not always know the will of God at any one time, by seeking His will in all that we do, including setting financial goals, God will direct our ways. I am sure that many of you at one time hoped for a change in career or job promotion, and were disappointed by not receiving it. After a period of time, another opportunity opened up that was significantly better than the previous one, and, if you had your way and taken the first position, you would have been disappointed.

By looking back on our lives, we can all see many instances in which God played a significant role in leading us to where we are today. Although we may look at this in the context of career or personal goals, we can also see the hand of God at work in our finances.

. . . .

Profession or Career

Everyone desires to make a difference, and to achieve something significant. That said, are you excited about waking up in the morning and going to work? If the statistics are reliable, depending on which statistic you read, about 60 to 80 percent of you do not like your job. According to the Billy Graham Evangelistic Association, 90 percent of Christians lead a defeated life. That is sad for us Americans who live in the land of opportunity. The question I would ask those of you who do not like your job is this: what are you doing to move toward a position in which you can be excited about getting up in the morning, passionate about the work you will do that day?

One of the principles I have always lived by is that life is too short to have a job that you hate, regardless of how much money it pays. One of my God-given blessings is that I have a job that I love and that fits my personality perfectly. This was not always the case.

For a long time I looked primarily at the money that I could make in the job, and not about getting a job that I loved to get up every day and do.

Changing my focus from how much money I made to what my passion is did not happen overnight; it was a process that I worked on for a number of years. Most Americans want instant results, and a longer-term process of moving toward a career that one can enjoy seems like too much work. I can assure you, however, that the benefits have been significant.

Some of the goals we focus on in this section are the industry we would like to work in, the company we would like to work for, the position level we are trying to achieve, and the pay we would like to obtain. If you are in sales, your goals may include the amount of sales you make each year, and even the possibility of owning your own business.

It is also important to reflect on God's direction and will for our vocational lives. Here are some passages that direct us not only to work, but to work hard:

Remember this: Whoever sows sparingly will also reap sparingly, and whoever sows generously will also reap generously (2 Corinthians 9:6).

Whatever your hand finds to do, do it with all your might, for in the grave, where you are going, there is neither working nor planning nor knowledge nor wisdom (Ecclesiastes 9:10).

He who works his land will have abundant food, but the one who chases fantasies will have his fill of poverty (Proverbs 28:19).

The hardworking farmer should be the first to receive a share of the crops (2 Timothy 2:6).

Note that in all of these passages of Scripture, God does not separate secular and sacred work. God states that our work should not only provide an income to support our basic needs, but also provide an opportunity to serve Him.

In addition, God's Word shows us that even though we may work for others, in reality, everything that we do is working for God.

> Whatever you do, work at it with all your heart, as working for the Lord, not for men (Colossians 3:23).

In addition to working hard and being cheerful in our vocations, God also calls us to be honest in our dealings, and to work with integrity.

> He who has been stealing must steal no longer, but must work, doing something useful with his own hands, that he may have something to share with those in need (Ephesians 4:28).

> For even when we were with you, we gave you this rule: "If a man will not work, he shall not eat" (2 Thessalonians 3:10).

> He who tends a fig tree will eat its fruit, and he who looks after his master will be honored (Proverbs 27:18).

In light of the many recent corporate scandals and the futile attempt by both governments and corporations to "bring back" ethical dealings, we are called, not by men, but by God to be ethical in all of our dealings and to be honest with our employers' resources.

It is also important to note that God wants us to enjoy our lives and career. Take note of the passage below:

> Then I realized that it is good and proper for a man to eat and drink, and to find satisfaction in his toilsome labor under the

sun during the few days of life God has given him—for this is his lot. Moreover, when God gives any man wealth and possessions, and enables him to enjoy them, to accept his lot and be happy in his work—this is a gift of God (Ecclesiastes 5:18-19).

There is an old saying that we need to work like it all depends on us, while trusting that the achievement of our goals will be a gift from God. God's will and plan need to be the central focus in these goals; our plans will not come to fruition if they are not God's goal for our lives.

For some of your career goals, you will need to list the additional resources such as time or education that would be needed to obtain that position.

In my case, I knew that I wanted to become a teacher. To do that I needed to go on for additional training, including the attainment of a Ph.D., which took a number of years to complete. For some of you, it may be important to develop a network of people who can begin to work with you and will help you in the future.

For example, if you would like to become a human resources director, you may want to develop a resource network that requires you to become a member of a society of human resources professionals, or a member of a CEO organization that would be full of people who would potentially hire you in the future.

Some of you may not know what career path to take, or what type of work you would enjoy doing. Thankfully, there are a number of instruments available through job training services, high school and college vocational counselors, or various Internet sites that can help you with this decision. One of these exceptional tests is the Campbell Interest and Skill Inventory (CISS), which is available from a number of sources, including the Internet.

If you are dissatisfied with your current position or pay, ask yourself, "Does God have the power to change my career, place of employment, or pay?" I am a firm believer that God does have this power. Yet, there must be a reason why you are in the position you are in, the company that you are at, and receiving the pay that you are receiving. I would encourage you to change your focus from the negative aspects of your job to why God has you in this position.

Some individuals have a goal of owning their own business. In fact, over the past decade, almost all of the growth in employment has come from smaller businesses. One area that you could explore is turning some of your activities or hobbies into a money-making venture.

I firmly believe that everyone should have multiple streams of income that can provide additional current income and be a buffer in case of job loss. These additional sources of income can lessen the blows of economic changes, and reduce the effects of globalization that many will experience. If we take a few moments we can all list a few things that we are already doing that we could turn into a business venture.

Interestingly, I was working with someone a few weeks ago who was unemployed and having a difficult time financially, who believed that God gave him a business idea. As he moved forward with this, it appeared very promising. The only explanation that he could suggest was that it was God-inspired. I know that if God inspires any of our plans, He will also not allow us to fail with them. In this case, I could not help but think that this again is God's way of providing for all of our needs.

With the benefits of technology, anyone can open a business from his bedroom or garage and make himself look as large as General Electric. If you have an interest in this area, I hope you continue to explore the benefits this could bring to you.

Your career is one of the most important aspects of providing personal significance in your life. Are you satisfied with how your career is progressing? If you are, what would make your life even better?

If not, what actions can you take in order to begin the process of moving toward God's plan for your life?

Are you enjoying your work? If not, what are you doing to move toward a career in which you can use your God-given talents in service to others? Take the time to review your list of career goals before you move on to the next section.

. . . .

Personal

Your goals in this section encompass your relationships with others, your emotional state, and the process of self-improvement. I am reminded of the Michael Jackson song *Man in the Mirror,* which in effect states that if you want to change the world, begin with yourself. There are those of us who may believe we are close to perfect. However, those who know us best not only know our limitations, but can also give us many suggestions for improvement. This feedback may at times be a painful reminder of how imperfect we are, but it will humble us as we try to improve.

Our friends are an important aspect of our personal relationships. Our friends share our joys and comfort us during times of grief. They congratulate us when we succeed and help us back up when we fall down.

How would you answer the following question: How many true friends do you have? Sort out your many acquaintances and focus on those who are most significant to you. Take the necessary time to develop your relationships with those whom you consider to be your true friends.

Another question: What specific actions have you taken in the last 30 days to further develop these true friendships? Perhaps you realize that many times you have taken these important relationships for granted. List a few goals for developing people skills that will improve your relationships with others.

Our emotional health also needs to be considered as part of our personal goals. Consider these thoughts from God's Word:

> For this very reason, make every effort to add to your faith goodness; and to goodness, knowledge; and to knowledge, self-control; and to self-control; perseverance; and to perseverance, godliness; and to godliness, brotherly kindness; and to brotherly kindness, love. For if you possess these qualities in increasing measure, they will keep you from being ineffective and unproductive in your knowledge of our Lord Jesus Christ (2 Peter 1:5-8).

God calls us to live a life of moral excellence, godliness, and self-control. This book has stressed that self-control must be exercised in order to control spending. Self-control is also important in our personal lives; it may require patience with the workings of God in our lives, and be a part of a genuine love of those around us.

Personal goals also need to include specific plans to enhance our knowledge and upgrade our skills. Consider these thoughts from the Word of God:

> Blessed is the man who finds wisdom, the man who gains understanding, for she is more profitable than silver and yields better returns than gold (Proverbs 3:13-14).

> The heart of the discerning acquires knowledge; the ears of the wise seek it out" (Proverbs 18:15).

> Wisdom is a shelter as money is a shelter, but the advantage of knowledge is this: that wisdom preserves the life of its possessor (Ecclesiastes 7:12).

But the wisdom that comes from heaven is first of all pure; then peace-loving, considerate, submissive, full of mercy and good fruit, impartial and sincere (James 3:17).

In times of an increasing globalization, individuals who stay ahead of others on the knowledge curve seem to always have an occupation. Unfortunately, spending an increasingly significant amount of time on unproductive activities such as watching television doesn't move anyone ahead in knowledge.

I believe increasing numbers of people know more about what is happening on the popular TV shows than they do about the changes going on within their career or the direction of the general economy. For some of you, the increase of knowledge may require you to attend additional classes in school. For everyone else, visiting the library or doing other research will help you upgrade your occupational skills.

Today, in the informational and digital age, just keeping abreast of the current developments will require increasing amounts of time and effort. College students in their junior and senior years may be studying facts that did not exist when they were freshman.

Ask yourself two questions as you develop goals in this area. First, what are you doing to make sure you are upgrading your knowledge within your field of work? Second, what could you be doing to significantly increase your knowledge?

For some of you, it may be as simple as turning off the television and picking up a book to read. For others, who are in a position that may be out-sourced in the next few years, it may mean setting goals toward achieving a new career. For even others, it may mean learning an additional language in order to remain competitive or moving to another country in order to provide a living for yourself and your family.

I am sure that as you develop goals within this section, you will find many opportunities to allow you to succeed in the future.

. . . .

Physical

To achieve the many goals that we have developed thus far, we need to be in good physical shape. Our bodies are called the temples of God, yet the rat race of daily existence has resulted in many eating fast food as we drive from appointment to appointment, or drinking on the weekends just to get away from life for a few hours.

Physical activity for many of us has become limited to typing on a keyboard or walking to and from our cars at work. Many of us may have health club memberships, but rarely use them because we are not able to get there because of our work schedules and time pressures. These memberships just become a wasted monthly expense. While this is not the case for all, it has become the norm for many Americans today.

All of this abuse of our bodies has taken a toll, and obesity and its related diseases are becoming more and more common. If you take the time to talk to someone who schedules time each week for physical activity, he will describe the benefits of this activity, and tell you how this has made him more productive in other areas of his life.

As you set goals for your physical health, consider what type of person you would like to become as a result of a particular habit or activity. What would you like to achieve, and how would this benefit you personally? Becoming physically fit may allow you to live longer and to spend more time with your spouse, children, and even your grandchildren! You may not see the benefit of exercise now, but taking a longer view will cause you to give physical activity a higher priority.

So, what type of physical goals should you set for yourself? That question depends on where you are physically and what form of physical fitness you believe you need to move forward. Based on your age, it may not be reasonable to expect that you will once again be able to achieve "six-pack" abs or a sculpted body.

It may be more reasonable to set a goal of getting a proper number of hours of rest each evening, or taking the stairs at work instead of the elevators. It may also be reasonable that we begin a smoking cessation plan, exercise routine, or a basic goal of not snacking on junk food between meals. For some, having a goal of losing an additional 20 lbs of weight may be a significant undertaking. For others, this may be a very reasonable and quickly achievable goal.

Lastly, it is important to remember that, before you act on any of your physical goals, you seek the advice of your doctor. He or she will help you focus on the goals that provide the greatest benefits, and advise you concerning additional action steps required to achieve greater success in this area.

What are the goals you have for your physical well-being? Take the time to list the goals you find important.

. . . .

Defining Needs Versus Wants

As you continue to develop your goals, be sure to understand the difference between needs and wants. Some goals involve necessities for our survival; others are simply things we would like to have or do. Maintaining a personal relationship with Jesus Christ should be a necessity. Retirement or funding our children's education may seem like a need, but more likely falls into the "want" category. We desire to fund our wants, but we need to ensure that we first have the resources to fund our more important and needful goals before we use limited financial resources to fund our wants.

. . . .

Writing Your Goals

As a financial planner, I often talk with people about their life goals. In many cases, people have developed some goals. Rarely have they written them down. It is crucial not only to take the time to write out your goals, but to post these goals in a very visible space in your home or office. (Just make sure that you don't post your career change goals where your boss can see them as this might accelerate your need to pursue that goal!)

Posting these goals becomes a constant reminder of what you value most in your life.

. . . .

Prioritizing Your Goals

Now it's time to prioritize your goals. Prioritize them on the basis of the time and resources that they will require. Unfortunately, you do not have unlimited time or financial resources that you can apply to your goals. Therefore, select goals that require your immediate focus, and leave other goals for the future should you gain additional resources.

It is important to remember that you can achieve any goal that you want. However, you will most likely not be able to achieve all of your goals. Does this mean we need to take some of our goals off our list? No, but be selective and focus your energy and resources on the ones that are most important to you.

You may determine that you have sufficient financial resources to achieve only the top three goals on your list. Although your children's education may be important to you, it may be number eight on the list. If it is not realistic to be able to achieve the goal of funding your children's education, you may need to inform them early on so they can focus on sports or getting good grades to increase their chance at getting scholarships. Or they may choose to take a job during high school to begin saving toward the cost of college. This may sound rather harsh, but it is part of prioritization. Remember, you can achieve almost any goal that you want . . . however, it is unlikely that you will be able to achieve or afford all of the goals that you set for yourself.

As you prioritize your goals, don't just consider your needs and desires. Be sure to include all of the individuals affected by the process. Other goals, such as new living room furniture, may be more important to your wife or your ministry of hospitality than the new bass boat that you want.

Sometime during this day, prioritize your goals and assign a priority number to each. Once you have completed this step, it may be helpful to re-list your goals in order of priority. The prioritization of your goals is a key step in the financial planning process—don't skimp on it!

. . . .

The Next Step: Action!

After you have prioritized your goals, it is time to make them a reality. Worksheet 14 provides assistance with implementing some of your high priority goals. You can list your high priority goals on this worksheet, and identify any potential obstacles that would prevent you from achieving them.

This worksheet also allows you to list potential partners who will hold you accountable as you work through this process and ensure that you stay on track. You can also specify the action steps you would need to take in order to make this goal a reality, and the time necessary for completing it.

For example, maybe one of your goals is going back for additional college education to prepare you for a new career. You can list the goal as "graduate with a bachelor's degree by 2015." Some action steps that you would need to take would be to investigate possible schools and complete an application. It may sound almost silly, but without taking the action of looking and applying, you will never achieve the educational goal that you have set.

Motivational speaker Anthony Robbins states that the clearer your goals are, the more powerful they will be, and the higher the level of success that you will have in achieving them.

. . . .

The Importance of Accountability

As you begin to achieve your goals, accountability and dedication to your goals become important. Each of us needs to have someone who holds us accountable and makes sure that we stick to the tasks that we have set for ourselves.

One of the things you will quickly find out is that one accountability partner may not be enough for each of your goals. You may want to look for and develop a relationship with someone who is spiritually mature who can help guide your journey toward your spiritual goals. You may need the assistance of a professional coach who can hold you accountable for your career goals and possibly hire a personal trainer to help you with your physical goals.

Remember that accountability can be as simple as having a spouse or personal friend ask you the right questions periodically as opposed to hiring a professional to guide your development and spending considerable funds to do it.

Regardless of which methods you choose, accountability is critical if you want to achieve your goals. Without some form of accountability, your goals may be nothing more than written dreams. Take the time to review your goals and decide on a person who could serve as your mentor and accountability partner for a minimum of one year.

It may also be helpful to designate an alternate person in case the primary person should turn you down. Take the time—do it now!

. . . .

Obtaining Godly Counsel

A key piece of advice that all of you can apply within your work today is the importance of getting godly counsel. The Bible has a number of passages that stress the importance of gaining godly counsel.

The way of a fool seems right to him, but a wise man listens to advice (Proverbs 12:15).

Plans fail for lack of counsel, but with many advisers they succeed (Proverbs 15:22).

Listen to advice and accept instruction, and in the end you will be wise (Proverbs 19:20).

A simple man believes anything, but a prudent man gives thought to his steps (Proverbs 14:15).

Make plans by seeking advice; if you wage war, obtain guidance (Proverbs 20:18).

Perfume and incense bring joy to the heart, and the pleasantness of one's friend springs from his earnest counsel. Do not forsake your friend and the friend of your father, and do not go to your brother's house when disaster strikes you—better a neighbor nearby than a brother far away (Proverbs 27:9-10).

It is the wise person who listens to others, and the fool who just goes his own way. Our plans and goals will only succeed through the power of God; we can gain much of this godly wisdom by listening to those who listen to Him.

One point that must be made is the power of having individuals around you who can support you, and counsel you from a number of points of view. You need to believe that you are the CEO of your life, and that you need to have a board of directors to provide guidance and direction.

Although these relationships may take years to develop, the time you invest in these godly relationships will pay off greatly for many years to come, and may even allow you to provide such a relationship to others.

. . . .

The Goal of Retirement

I am sure that some of you dream of a time when you can retire and relax in a warm tropical climate instead of engaging in the daily stress and grind of work. Although some of you are planning to work well into your sixties or seventies, others may want to retire much earlier. Either way, we need to realize that we may be either forced into retirement or given the opportunity of retiring early. Retirement is not something you can just wake up one morning and do. Take a look at some of these Biblical instructions from the book of Proverbs:

Go to the ant, you sluggard; consider its ways and be wise! It has no commander, no overseer or ruler, yet it stores its provisions in summer and gathers its food at harvest. How long will you lie there, you sluggard? When you will get up from your sleep? A little sleep, a little slumber, a little folding of the hands to rest (Proverbs 6:6-10).

Retirement is a goal that must be carefully considered throughout your entire life. Based on knowledge of the time value of money (covered in an upcoming chapter), you will learn that the sooner you start saving for retirement, the lower the amount of money you will need to save each month.

Depending on your desired level of income at retirement, if you would start putting money away at twenty years of age, the amount you would need to put away would only be a few hundred dollars per month. However, if you wait to save for retirement until your mortgage is paid off, and the kids have been through college, you may have to put away many thousands per month.

PRACTICAL EXAMPLE

Ben Smith, age 50, wants to begin saving for retirement. He would like to retire at age 65 and, based on his calculations, needs to have a total savings of $3 million by then. To achieve his goal, at a 10 percent return, he would need to save $7,178 per month or $86,140 per year. If Ben had started this savings program when he was 20, his monthly amount would have been $284 per month.

Some of you may be thinking that it would have been great to start saving for retirement at twenty, but you are in your late forties or early fifties and are wondering what to do now. That is an excellent question to which there are relatively few answers. The reality of this situation is that you may have to accept a greatly reduced standard of living, retire much later than you had hoped, or plan to work as long as you are able.

Again, by not planning, your options at this stage of your life are greatly reduced. If you are asking why someone has not told you about this previously, all I can say is that many people do not think about the future when there is so much happening in the present. However, a number of factors are starting to change this thinking. These will be discussed next.

. . . .

Current State of Retirement

Retirement is currently perceived as a period of time that is a reward for many years of working. Current retirees have the benefits of a long life span, pensions, Social Security, and higher than average personal savings as many of them learned the importance of personal savings going through the Depression.

Let's look at this in greater detail. When we talk about retirement, we often talk about the three important legs of the retirement stool: personal savings, pensions, and Social Security. Most retirees today experienced the effects of the Great Depression, which caused them to be one of the generations that saved the most.

Many of these individuals lived in the industrial age when pension programs were the norm, and many of them are currently receiving monthly benefit checks from their former employers.

In addition, many of these individuals did not contribute greatly to Social Security based upon much lower life expectancy norms when the program was created.

When you consider all of these facts, you would think that the average retiree is very wealthy. In reality, only a small minority of current retirees earn more than $50,000 per year, with the majority of them earning less than $20,000 per year.

The changes in interest rates over the past few years have had a great effect upon current retirees; and the changes in interest rates benefit the people who have mortgages, but individuals on fixed incomes saw substantial reductions in their incomes as the interest rates fell.

These considerations, however, are nothing compared to challenges the next generation of retirees will face!

. . . .

Changes in Retirement Planning

One of the major challenges of retirement today is for the Baby Boomer population. The Baby Boomers were born between 1946 and 1964 and represent 78 million Americans or 27.5 percent of the population of the United States. More than 33 million of them are over 50 years old, and many of them have not sufficiently planned for their retirement. Tomorrow's retirees will face a set of challenges including increased life spans, additional changes to Social Security benefits, changes in pension plans, and lack of personal savings.

Although there has been some talk within the federal government about the problems the Social Security system will likely face, little is being done by Congress to address these potential challenges. Based on projections made by the Social Security Administration, in 2017 it will begin paying more in benefits than is collected through Social Security taxes, and by 2041 the Social Security Trust Fund will be exhausted. Social Security then will only be able to pay 75 cents for each dollar of scheduled benefits.

Why is this not being addressed by today's politicians? Most of these changes are going to happen after the current politicians leave office. They are not worried about problems that may occur in the future and are only concerned about dealing with the backlash this issue would raise.

There are a number of questions that arise when you consider what Social Security covers, and what it doesn't. Social Security pays retirement, disability, family, and survivor benefits. In addition, Medicare, a government program often associated with Social Security, pays for health expenses for inpatient hospital care, nursing care, doctors' fees, medication, and other medical services and supplies for citizens sixty-five and older, as well as the people who have been receiving disability benefits through Social Security.

When can you receive your benefits? Based on current Social Security regulations, if you were born before 1938, you can retire with full benefits at age 65. In 1983, a change in the law caused the full retirement age to gradually increase to age 67 for people born after 1960. However, regardless of how old you are, you can retire as early as age 62, and take benefits at a reduced rate. If you work beyond your full retirement age, you can receive higher benefits based on additional earnings and credits.

As we look at the history of Social Security, we will quickly realize that Social Security was never intended to be the sole provider of retirement income, nor was it intended to provide benefits for the life spans that we are now enjoying. When Social Security was introduced, one normally retired at 62 and died at 67. First recipients of Social Security Benefits were typically on the program for only five years. Compare that to today's retiree who retires at 62 and is on Social Security for 25 years or more.

A significant shift also has occurred in the retirement benefits offered by many major corporations. For many years, the defined benefit plan, or pension, was the benefit of choice. At one time there were over 100,000 defined benefit plans. Today, this number has dwindled to less than 30,000 as more and more companies are opting for the more contributory format that is used in many of the 401(k) plans.

There are a number of good reasons for this. For many years, companies have assumed the investment risk when they guaranteed the benefits that were to be provided by the plan. This investment risk reduced employers' earnings when markets were down, as the company was required to make up any amount when their plans were underfunded due to market decline; these contributions were taken directly from the earnings of the company.

Employees also liked the shift. Employees were changing employers more and more frequently and never were able to earn a substantial benefit from these traditional pension plans. They are happier to have a more portable retirement plan that can be transferred from employer to employer. Since many of these participants were younger, they also believed that by investing their retirement funds in a more aggressive manner, they could get a higher level of return than what was available from their employer, thus providing a higher standard of living at retirement.

Another challenge is a lack of personal savings for the next generation of retirees. Most of the future Baby Boomer retirees have lived through a generation of excessive spending. By some accounts, this generation spends more than we have ever seen in the United States. Interestingly, according to statistics from the Bureau of Labor and Statistics the average amount of retirement savings was $49,922; however the median amount was only $2,000. This same source reported that the average amount of financial assets was $101,518, far short of what most people need for their savings. In fact, when you ask many people about their level of savings, most just pull out their wallet. This level of personal savings will not support an adequate level of retirement income.

When confronted by these facts, many Baby Boomers state that they will just have to work longer in the jobs that they currently have. Unfortunately for them, this may not be an option. Due to the many changes that globalization and the digital age are bringing about, many of the current jobs may no longer exist in another 20 years, and the Baby Boomers may not have the necessary skills to compete on a global scale with younger or possibly foreign individuals for these positions.

. . . .

The Goal of Becoming Debt-Free

The dream and goal of being debt-free can be achieved! One of the goals every individual or family reading this book should have is to become debt-free. Now that you have some of the tools, becoming debt-free can be achieved by anyone who will take the time, and persevere toward this goal.

If you make this goal a priority, you will begin to look at some of your expenditures and choose whether to make a purchase for immediate gratification or to be debt-free more quickly. Many individuals make other investments before they are debt-free. Any investment has associated risks, and making investments too early may slow the process of becoming debt-free.

Tomorrow we will be looking at these possible investments and their associated risks. Today, let's just make sure that we have a good handle on the goals that we would like to achieve in this life. Take the time to complete all of these previous activities now before moving forward.

Summary and Application

Today we set out on the exciting journey of developing appropriate goals for each of the major areas of our lives. We developed spiritual, family, financial, professional or career, personal, and physical goals. Goals are powerful in our lives. Well-developed goals in each of these areas help to ensure that our lives are balanced.

It is important that you continually develop short-term as well as longer range goals to keep your focus on both the present and the future. One of the ways you can develop these goals would be to review the needs and wants that you have for your life. It is important to prioritize our goals to ensure that our financial resources will be directed where they are most needed.

It is also important to write out your goals because written goals have a far better chance of being achieved. Using written goals will start a force within us that will almost certainly ensure success within our lives. Yet, written goals without the commitment to take action on them are worthless. Make the commitment!

Once you have developed appropriate goals, you need to take appropriate action and continually work toward them. Even though successful achievement of your goals is dependent on God's direction for your life, you still need to work as though you are the one responsible.

One strategy for both developing these goals and moving toward successful completion of them is to garner godly counsel and accountability. Prayer and God's leading ensure that you are on the right path!

One of the major goals that we all have is the goal of retirement. Retirement in the future may be very different from what is it now due to a number of demographic factors. The goal of retirement needs to be appropriately planned for, and we cannot wait for government action or governmental support during this period of life.

Becoming debt-free is another goal that we each need to include in our set of personal and financial goals.

Action Steps for Today

- Using the appropriate provided forms, develop two to three short-term goals within each of the goal areas (Worksheets 13 and 14).
- Using the appropriate provided forms, develop six to seven long-term goals within each of the goal areas (Worksheets 13 and 14).
- Use the Web tools to determine the cost of your retirement based on the retirement date you have set.
- Ensure that one of your goals is to become debt-free.
- Using the goal development form, spell out your goals in detail, determine the resources that would be needed to achieve your goals, and consider any potential obstacles you may encounter in achieving your goals.

DAY **6**

. . . .

investing to meet your goals

To achieve the goals we developed yesterday, we will need to make effective short- and long-term investment decisions. Unfortunately, no matter how carefully we consider our investments and the markets, there is no guarantee of a positive return. Therefore, it is important that we understand the various available options, and then choose one or more strategies that both fit our time frame and are most likely to provide the funds we need when we need them.

Among other things, today we will develop an understanding of how the financial markets work, and how you can set up your first investment account. It is not the intent of this day to make you an expert investor. Rather, the goal is to lay a foundation on which you can build.

Although much of what we are covering today could become quite technical, one of my goals is to present this information in an effective and understandable manner.

. . . .

Biblical Perspectives on Investing

Throughout this book, we have actively used solid biblical principles for financial guidance. The same is true today. Consider this passage from the book of Ecclesiastes:

> I have seen a grievous evil under the sun: wealth hoarded to the harm of its owner, or wealth lost through some misfortune, so that when he has a son there is nothing left for him (Ecclesiastes 5:13-14).

Biblically, our goal in investing isn't to gain riches or earthly prosperity. Rather, it is to provide for ourselves, to provide for the opportunities for service that God gives to us, and to leave something for those who will stay on this earth after we depart.

Of course, the financial press often promotes worldly views of wealth creation. Our investments will make us wealthy only if God allows this to happen. We need to continually seek God's will throughout this process, since everything we have belongs to Him.

. . . .

Eternal Investing or Personal Future

An important aspect of investing we need to consider is whether to invest for this world, or to invest for eternal returns. Take 30 seconds to read these passages from Proverbs and Ecclesiastes:

Honor the LORD with your wealth, with the firstfruits of all your crops; then your barns will be filled to overflowing, and your vats will brim over with new wine (Proverbs 3:9-10).

In the house of the wise are stores of choice food and oil, but a foolish man devours all he has (Proverbs 21:20).

Give portions to seven, yes to eight, for you do not know what disaster may come upon the land (Ecclesiastes 11:2).

Yes, I realize some quote these passages to promote their own prosperity theories: "If we give more to God, we'll receive untold wealth in return." Now, God may cause our prosperity to increase over time, or He may bless us in other ways such as good health or positive relationships. Not all blessings that we will receive may be financial. However, it is important that we place our complete trust in *God*, not someone's theories or promises.

From Scripture it's quite clear that God doesn't promise to make everyone rich. Even Jesus said there will always be some who are poor. What God promises to provide is everything we *need*.

However, an important point can be made from these Scripture passages: The money God gives us should not be spent only to meet our current needs. Instead, a portion of our income should be given to God and another portion should be saved for the future. After all, if we spend everything for today, we'll have nothing for the future and may not be able to accomplish what God has planned for us.

. . . .

The Fruitlessness of Trying to Become Rich

It might sound great to be rich, but wealth comes with its own sets of problems and issues and probably wouldn't make us any happier than we are now. When I look around at the abundant resources most of us have, I question how happy most of us really are.

Then again, as I travel the world and see those with so little, it continually impresses me how many are genuinely happy. This is especially true of our brothers and sisters in Christ, even in the poorest of nations. The celebrations in their church services would put many of our church services to shame. They truly know what it is to trust God and praise Him with all their hearts.

The Bible is quite clear that it is fruitless to strive to become rich here on earth. Take a moment to read these brief passages from Proverbs and 1 Timothy:

> Do not wear yourself out to get rich; have the wisdom to show restraint. Cast but a glance at riches, and they are gone, for they will surely sprout wings and fly off to the sky like an eagle (Proverbs 23:4-5).

> People who want to get rich fall into temptation and a trap and into many foolish and harmful desires that plunge men into ruin and destruction. For the love of money is a root of all kinds of evil. Some people, eager for money, have wandered from the faith and pierced themselves with many griefs (1 Timothy 6:9-10).

If God allows us to become rich, it's clear that we need to have the appropriate attitude toward these riches or they will disappear. It's happened all through history right down to our day.

How many people do you know who were hurt by the dot.com bust a decade ago? And how many more people do you know who suffered huge losses in the wake of the recent credit and stock market meltdowns?

God often uses events like these to bring our focus back where it needs to be—on Him, and Him alone!

. . . .

Get-Rich-Quick Schemes

As I look at the covers of business and financial magazines, and as I watch infomercials on television, it's apparent that a lot of people want to sell me something to make me rich. Some claim that we can make millions in just a few hours a month using their real estate techniques, or make thousands every week by buying and selling stocks using their technical reports.

Of course, most Americans realize the people selling these products are the only ones getting rich, while those who buy their products often get farther and farther behind financially. "Get-rich-quick" schemes are just that—schemes to get their hands on your hard-earned money.

I probably have seen almost every possible scheme out there. These include many real estate programs, multi-level marketing opportunities, oil field investments, and investment trading systems using technical charting, options, and foreign currency.

I always asked myself: If this system makes money so easily, why are they trying to sell it to me? Why wouldn't they want to keep it a secret or use it themselves to make untold millions?

Of course, every scheme has a few success stories. But what's the average person's experience? Money out, more money out, little or no money back. Their advice: Work harder, work smarter, network more, spend more. After all, "your turn's next." It's a lie. There is no such thing as a "get-rich-quick" *system*. Only schemes.

Am I saying all of these systems do not work? No, but most of them require hard work—over many years—to learn the system and profit from it. There are much better uses of your time and money, believe me.

Better yet, consider these wise words from the book of Proverbs:

A stingy man is eager to get rich and is unaware that poverty awaits him (Proverbs 28:22).

. . . .

Is It a Sin to Be Rich?

Sadly, it's popular to knock the rich, to criticize them, and even to judge them. On top of that, a number of wealthy Christians do feel guilty about having worldly wealth. I believe much of this guilt comes from misunderstanding the Scripture passage where Jesus states it is easier for a camel to go through an eye of a needle than for a rich man to enter the kingdom of God.

Let's not forget that his followers included both rich women (like Joanna and Susanna, Luke 8:1-4) and rich men (like Zacchaeus, Luke 19:1-10). Wealth is not the problem—it's our attitude toward riches that's critical. As we've seen earlier, the love of money is the root of all kinds of evil.

Our responsibility is to not strive for riches or feel guilty about the wealth God gives us; rather, our responsibility is to take into account God's purposes, take care of ourselves, and be a proper steward of these resources.

Take a look at these passages from Scripture:

But remember the LORD your God, for it is he who gives you the ability to produce wealth, and so confirms his covenant, which he swore to your forefathers, as it is today (Deuteronomy 8:18).

The wicked man earns deceptive wages, but he who sows righteousness reaps a sure reward (Proverbs 11:18).

If all Christians today were poor, how would God accomplish His purposes in the world? I believe God uses us as a channel to funnel His blessings through us to those who are in need. When we are faithful with the resources we have, I believe God blesses us and often gives us more. As He provides more, we can give more. Wealth for us may be nothing more than a sign of God's blessing so we can be a blessing to others.

Granted, it's easy for someone who becomes wealthy to change his attitude. Instead of depending on God, one can become self-reliant. These illusions of self-reliance lead them to believe they can do whatever they want, and do it without God's help. Such illusions, however, are in direct conflict with God's will for our lives.

It's easy for someone to hoard his or her assets. Such hoarding, instead of trusting God to provide, is a common occurrence today. While we are wise to have a surplus for future needs, hoarding wealth—instead of blessing others with it—is contrary to God's revealed plan.

The money we have is not our own. It is a resource to use as God reveals to us how to use it. Let us never make the mistake of thinking our personal efforts have generated the wealth we enjoy. Any wealth we have is from the hand of God.

Over the years I have met many individuals I would consider quite rich. It is often amazing to see how they change over time. And their wealth often changes, too. Some end up in serious financial trouble.

If God blesses us with riches, we should be thankful and use these God-given resources to bless others. If God chooses not to bless us with riches, we still should be thankful, grateful, and content with all of the resources and blessings we do have.

. . . .

Understanding the Time Value of Money

One of the most foundational principles of finance is the time value of money.

We all know that money invested over time grows not only from the interest you receive, but also on the compounding of the interest you already have received.

The time value of money can be seen in other ways, too. Which would you rather have: $20 today or $20 twenty years from now? I'm pretty sure you would choose $20 today, and you would make the correct choice.

A number of problems are listed in this section to serve as an example of how the principle of the time value of money applies to our finances and the achievement of our goals. The calculations in this section can be performed easily using a calculator that has financial functions (one of them is the TI-83, which is what most teenagers use in school). If you do not have access to this calculator, you can find financial calculators in office supply stores, you can use functions in Microsoft Excel, or you can use any of a number of online Web sites that allow individuals to perform financial calculations.

Here are some sample problems with solutions:

1) How much would you have if you invested $10,000 today, left it in an account for 40 years, and earned 10 percent interest? The answer to this problem is $452,592.26. That is a very large sum of money accumulated in over four decades. Instead, how much money would you have if you used the

$10,000 to purchase a car? After *far* fewer than 40 years of use the car would be worth nearly $0.

2) Will the difference of a few percentage points in the interest return you receive make that much of a difference? Let's say you have $10,000 today and invest it at 2, 4, 6, 8, 10, or 12 percent interest. Here are the amounts you would have in 35 years:

- 2 percent return $ 19,998.90
- 4 percent return $ 39,460.89
- 6 percent return $ 76,860.87
- 8 percent return $147,853.33
- 10 percent return $281,024.37
- 12 percent return $527,996.20

As you can see, there is a *significant* difference in the amounts you would have. It is important to remember these differences don't require you to work any harder; rather, it is your money working harder for you.

As you also will note, to get the higher returns you probably won't keep your money in a bank or other lower risk investments. Instead, you'll need to invest in things that provide a higher return. To get higher returns, therefore, you also have to be willing to incur a correspondingly higher risk.

3) What if every year you have another $4,000 to invest for the next 35 years? Here is how much you would have at the end of the 35 years:

- 2 percent return $ 203,977.47
- 4 percent return $ 306,393.26
- 6 percent return $ 472,483.47
- 8 percent return $ 744,408.59
- 10 percent return $1,192,507.22
- 12 percent return $1,933,852.46

A small amount of money invested appropriately on a regular basis can provide significant returns in the future.

4) If you want to start a business in 20 years at a startup cost of $50,000, you could either deposit $8,320.64 as a lump sum today or $74.31 per month in order to meet this goal, assuming you could obtain a 9 percent investment return.

5) I like to joke that there is only one thing worse than dying, and that is to outlive your money. Let's assume you are 40 years old, you want to retire at age 60, and you plan on living until 95 years of age. Although this may seem like a particularly long lifespan, with all of the advances in modern medical technology it's a more likely lifespan than most people realize. Then again, if I'm wrong, you'll die with plenty of money.

Let's assume you want to earn $50,000 per year in today's dollars for retirement. If you earn 8 percent on your investments, but inflation runs 3.5 percent, the amount you'll need to have saved by retirement is $1,849,391.27.

If you started at age 20 to meet this goal, you would need to save $1,047.13 per month. At age 30 the amount is $1,738.82. If your current age is 40, however, the amount is $3,118.98, and if you wait until you are 50 years old, the amount is a whopping $7,118.96 per month.

You may be thinking, *Where am I going to get that kind of money from my current budget?* There is no easy method. We simply have to choose what we will do without today in order to have what we will need in the future.

The time value of money also can be used to determine the true costs of some of our habits. Let's assume a potential return of 10 percent on your money. If you drink $4.50 worth of coffee daily at Starbucks for your entire working career, you've lost $626,848.29 in retirement funds. If you smoke one $5.00 pack of cigarettes a day, the cost over 40 years is $977,888.35. If you purchase lottery tickets at a rate of $50 per week, you've forfeited the opportunity to be a millionaire in well under 40 years.

Life is full of choices, and the money we spend today may limit some of our choices in the future. The reverse is also true. You can make very small daily sacrifices and still reap huge rewards when you reach retirement age. Also, just think about the immense amount of time you'll save not standing in line all the time.

. . . .

Understanding Your Personal Risk Tolerance

Before making any investments, it is important that you take the time to assess your personal risk tolerance. In addition, if you are married, you need to assess the personal risk tolerance of your spouse. During all of my years of managing investments for couples, I have never found a husband and wife who shared the same level of risk tolerance. Instead, I have often commented that it's funny how often God puts two individuals together who are almost polar opposites with respect to their risk tolerances.

So, before we go any further, how would you describe your risk tolerance? If the stock market declined 40 percent tomorrow, what would be your reaction? Would you say now is one of the best times to invest? Would you sell everything to get out of the market? Or would you simply hold on to what you have and not invest any more?

Each of these options describes a different tolerance for risk. Some individuals tend to be very aggressive, and take considerable risks in order to get greater returns on their money. Some others are very conservative. For them investing in the stock market is perceived as too risky, and they feel much safer leaving their assets in banks or government investments. Neither approach is wrong.

Knowing your personal risk tolerance is important for two reasons. First, it will help you not to make investments which pose risks that exceed your tolerance. I am a firm believer that greater investment returns are not worth daily worry and sleepless nights. You have to choose what's right for you. Second, knowing your risk tolerance can increase your returns by allowing you to use asset allocation models, which I'll explain later.

To determine your risk tolerance, you need to ask yourself the following question: How much loss in the value of my investments would cause me concern at this stage of my life?

If you are older with minimal savings, you may not have any tolerance for risk and would be concerned if you lost any of the value of your investments. If you are younger with many years of work ahead of you, you may be willing to take on greater risks in the hope of getting greater returns.

With today's relatively volatile interest rates, individuals on a fixed income often take greater risks to maintain the same level of income. Although that may seem like an effective investment strategy, they also need to be concerned with the quality of their investments. Remember these days it is not the return *on* the investment that's important; rather, it is the return *of* the investment that's critical! It is useless to have a 20 percent annual return on your investment only to lose everything six years from now. Always heed this sound advice from investment guru Warren Buffett of Berkshire Hathaway:

Rule #1: Don't lose money.
Rule #2: Don't forget Rule #1.

. . . .

Your First Investment

One of the questions I am often asked is, "What is the best investment I should make at this point?" After much thought, I finally arrived at the world's most perfect investment. Here are some of the characteristics of this investment:

- Fits into virtually anyone's personal risk tolerance
- Has an incredible *guaranteed* return of between 13 and 30 percent per year
- Can be made by anyone (without the help of investment brokers, financial advisors, or other professionals).
- Can have any amount invested in any given month (even $5 makes a difference). Interested in this investment? I hope so! All you need to do is start paying off your credit cards. With the average U.S. household carrying up to $9,000 in credit card debt, you're absolutely best investment is paying off that debt. The return you will receive over time will be substantially higher than any other investment you can make.

Before you invest one dollar elsewhere, it's a must: Pay off your credit cards!

. . . .

Your Second Investment

After paying off your credit cards, the next investment you should make is to set up an emergency fund. Emergencies include losing your job or incurring huge medical bills.

Emergencies don't include replacing the roof of your house or repairing your car, which are normal expenses that should be anticipated and funded by the savings accounts you will set up within your budget.

How big should your emergency fund be? Ideally, it should cover all of your essential expenses for six months (once you factor in your state's unemployment benefits). That sounds like a lot, but the reality is it could take more than half a year to find a new job.

Your initial goal for an emergency fund, though, should be enough to cover expenses for a month. Once you reach that level, focus on saving enough for three months. Then continue until you have six months covered.

Of course, the real goal is up to you. The total you put in this emergency fund will depend in part on how long you want to be protected, the relative availability of jobs within your area, your preferred lifestyle, and your ability to change your lifestyle quickly should the need arise.

Where should these emergency funds be held? Options include money market accounts, savings accounts, or short-term bank CDs. The most important consideration is that your funds are at no risk of being lost. The next consideration is some form of return— although, if you use a savings account, this return may be quite small. Even if the return is small, you want to make sure the funds always will be there in case of emergency.

. . . .

Considering New Investment Options

Once you have your credit cards paid off and have established a sizeable emergency fund, it's time to move into the third stage of investing, which includes investing in financial securities. Before we proceed with these types of investments, it is important to gain some knowledge of the various investment options, the strategies currently used by investors for managing these invested funds, how the financial markets work, and the various types of accounts we can establish. This section of Day 6 focuses on these critical investment factors.

. . . .

Separating Investment Vehicles from Investments

Often people are confused about investing because they don't understand the difference between actual investments and the vehicles or types of accounts used to make these investments.

We will first focus on the various types of investments we can make. We need to understand, though, that these investments can be made in a variety of different accounts; these various types of accounts can be reviewed in the book's supplementary Web site, www.sevendaymakeover.com.

For example, consider the following: Can you invest in stocks with an Individual Retirement Account (IRA)? Stocks can be purchased in a variety of account types. An IRA is one vehicle or type of account used to make such investments.

. . . .

Understanding Investment Options

Investments in today's financial world are becoming more and more complex. Also, the wide array of products offered by hundreds of financial institutions can become very confusing if we're not careful.

In most cases, investment products are not designed to be confusing. But all the features added to and offered with these products today (largely in response to customer requirements and needs) can quickly overwhelm the new investor. Add the necessary components of proper investment portfolio construction and eyes tend to glaze over...just as yours are doing now! So you can better understand some of the available options, however, I want to give you a fairly simple framework you can use from here on out.

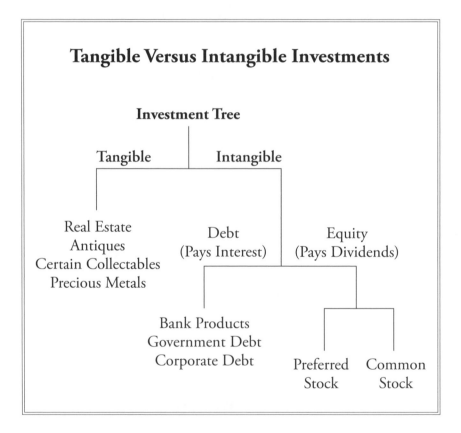

As you look at the investment tree above, you will see that it differentiates between tangible and intangible investments. Tangible investments are investments are investments you can see and feel, and you can often see their value. Investments in this category include homes, real estate, certain antiques and collectables, and precious metals such as gold and platinum.

Although you might guess that automobiles would fall into this category, they don't because they virtually always depreciate in value over time (unless they're a collectable).

Another tangible investment includes Real Estate Investment Trusts (REITS), which act like mutual funds but invest in shopping malls, office buildings, retirement complexes, and other forms of real estate. Although these investments are not often included in a portfolio, they offer an additional dimension that should be considered.

In his best-selling book *Rich Dad...Poor Dad*, Robert Kiyosaki noted that 97 percent of self-made millionaires became millionaires through real estate. If you look at that statistic alone, I believe you will agree that investments in real estate should be considered in any portfolio.

On the right side of the investment tree, we see various types of intangible investments. They are called intangible investments because we cannot touch or feel the value the security holds. Take a $1 bill from your wallet or purse and look at it. How much is this $1 bill worth? (This is not a trick question.) It's worth a dollar, of course. If I pay someone with a $1 bill, I receive a dollar's worth of goods or services in return.

Now look at this page closely. Can you tell me the difference between this page and the paper used in the $1 bill? You might say the paper used in the $1 bill is better, and therefore worth more than this page. Okay, then take a $20 bill out of your wallet and tell me the difference between the $1 and the $20 bill. I think you get the point!

The dollar bill is a piece of paper that has value because of who printed on it and what they printed, and because of those factors you will accept it as payment. Throughout history, many things have been used as currency, including metals, spices, shells, sand, rocks, massive carved stones, and even tulip bulbs. All someone needs is an accepted medium of exchange, and the payment process can occur.

. . . .

Debt Investments

Intangible investments come in the form of debt or equity. Simply stated, any debt investment is a loan to someone else for a period of time. The return you receive for making this investment is interest.

One of the easiest ways to understand this type of investment is your home or car payments in reverse. Someone loaned you money that you used to purchase your home or car, and each month you are paying back part of the principal and all of that month's interest to that individual or entity. Of course, there are a number of types of debt instruments.

First, any type of bank product is a debt investment. When you put money into a checking or savings account or into a CD, you are loaning this money to the bank for a period of time. For the privilege of having this money to loan out to others, the bank often agrees to pay you interest in return, although typically a very small amount.

Second, any type of government note, bill, or bond is a loan to the government and the "investor" receives a specific amount of interest over time. Most U.S. government investments today are considered safe because there is such a small risk of default (because the government can always print more money if necessary). Because these investments have so little risk, they don't earn a lot of interest over time. Subsequently, very few people invest in government bonds, but the government still needs to borrow funds. Therefore, a lot of U.S. bonds are sold to foreign countries, which may cause some huge problems in the future. As Proverbs says, the borrower serves the lender.

The ***third*** type of debt investments is loaning money to munici-palities. Many municipalities borrow money to cover part of their budget or to finance convention centers, sports venues, and other large community projects. Often these municipal or "muni" bonds offer tax-free returns on both the state and federal level. As a result, interest rates tend to be relatively low. Still, they're an investment worth actively considering.

Should someone consider investing in municipal bonds, though, specifically to avoid paying higher income taxes? The answer is quite simple and depends on the individual's marginal income tax rate (the amount of tax on the next dollar of earnings).

Let's look at the results for individuals in the 15, 28, and 35 per-cent federal tax brackets. We will assume that the interest rate of a corporate bond is 5 percent, and the return on the municipal is only 3 percent. We will also assume a 5 percent state income tax. Here's what would happen if someone purchased a $1,000 corporate bond within each federal tax bracket:

	35 percent	*28 percent*	*15 percent*
Corporate bond interest	$50.00	$50.00	$50.00
Federal income tax	$17.50	$14.00	$ 7.50
State Income tax	$ 2.50	$ 2.50	$ 2.50
Total tax	$20.00	$16.50	$10.00
After-tax gain	**$30.00**	**$33.50**	**$40.00**
Municipal bond interest	$30.00	$30.00	$30.00
Difference	*$0.00*	*$3.50*	*$10.00*

As you can see, most individuals can get a higher return by pur-chasing a corporate bond and paying the required income taxes. Municipal bonds are generally beneficial only for those in the high-est income tax bracket.

The ***fourth*** type of debt investment is loaning money to corpo-rations. Many corporate entities borrow money on a regular basis to finance short-term seasonal or cyclical needs, and to finance long-term needs for capital projects or equipment (including production lines, airplanes, or ships).

In order to understand these investments better, some definitions may be helpful:

- *Maturity date:* The date on which, if you make the loan, you would get your money back.
- *Coupon rate:* The rate of return that you would receive on your investment. For example, if the rate was 5 percent, you would receive $50 per year for every $1,000 you invested.
- *Yield to maturity:* The actual return you would receive on your investment if you held the bond until maturity.
- *Bond risks:* The risk that you will not receive your initial investment amount (principle) back in the case of a corporate default or bankruptcy. For example, investors in companies like Enron, General Motors, or WorldCom a few years ago probably received a fairly high rate of interest, but they also faced a higher risk of not getting their money back. (I want to emphasize again that it is not the return *on* the investment that is most important; instead, it's the return *of* the investment!)
- *Bond provisions:* There are a number of provisions that can be, and often are, included with the purchase of a bond. These provisions are call and conversion provisions, which will be defined more fully below.
- *Call privileges:* These are an important consideration for investors for a number of reasons. Call provisions are rights given to the issuer (loaner) that allow him to pay back the loan at various times specified in the agreement. This may sound appealing to the issuer but you, as the loaner, may get your money back when interest rates are low, causing you to purchase a new investment at a much higher level of risk in order to get the same amount of return. This is called reinvestment risk. If the loaner has this privilege, the

loaner will pay a higher rate of interest.

- *Bond conversions:* This allows the loaner (corporation) to convert bonds for stock based on the details of the original loan agreement. This may protect the loaner from its stock going up rapidly, or the quality of its bond deteriorating. As well, a company may do this to ensure that its bonds are sold and generally will pay a higher rate of interest.

Some debt investments, including bank products, are stable. The value of others, including longer term government and corporate bonds, can change based on the relative health of the economy, the strengths and weaknesses of the company, and interest rate fluctuations.

Some individuals try to gauge interest rate fluctuations in an attempt to profit from them. When Alan Greenspan was chairman of the Federal Reserve Board, some investors would look at how he was holding his briefcase on the day the Federal Reserve was scheduled to announce rates changes. Some claimed that if he was holding his briefcase with all five fingers it was heavy, which meant the Federal Reserve was going to do something with the rates. If he held his briefcase with only two fingers, investors thought there would be no change and the markets would trade normally. This may sound ridiculous, but investors regularly attempt to profit from such hunches.

The *final* type of debt investments we can make is in foreign governments or foreign corporations. While the interest rate returns on these types of investments are often appealing, there are additional risks. Those additional risks include political issues, currency fluctuations, and other factors that must be taken into account.

If you are able to get a 14 percent return on a New Zealand bond, yet the American dollar strengthens against the New Zealand dollar by 18 percent, the return would be negative 4 percent. Then again, if the American dollar weakens, the return could be huge.

Now, we turn from one form of intangible investments to another type.

. . . .

Equity Investments

On the investment tree above, you see both preferred stocks and common stocks included on the equity side. Equity investments represent the ownership we have in a company. As an owner, we do not receive interest on our investment. Instead, our return is paid in the form of dividends.

Preferred stock is considered a hybrid security since it contains many of the components of bonds, including a stated dividend rate and maturity. Preferred stock gets its name from having a preference over common stock for dividends and assets should the company go into bankruptcy. There is usually less volatility in the prices of preferred stock, even though it is an equity investment and there is no guarantee you will receive a dividend.

A number of provisions can be added to preferred stock. One is being callable like some debt investments. Other provisions can include being paid before any dividends are paid to shareholders of common stock, and allowing preferred stockholders to receive additional earnings in times of significant corporate earnings (instead of common shareholders receiving all of the benefits).

Simply stated, common stock is straight ownership in a company. A few years ago, one brokerage firm ran an advertisement featuring a kid showing up for baseball practice and telling his coach that his dad owned Nike. The coach has a vision of all of the kids in brand-new uniforms in a new stadium, all sporting the Nike logo. A few seconds later, the dad shows up with ketchup dripping down his Nike T-shirt, which noted his name and 0.00000000001 percent ownership of Nike.

This ad tried to prove a point. It was also an exceptional example of what company ownership is. If you purchase 500 shares of stock in a company like Nike, and there are 500 million total company shares, you would own a millionth of the company, and have a right to a millionth of the company's profits. You may not be able to say you own all of the door hinges or the sign out front of Nike's international headquarters in Beaverton, Oregon. Instead, you would own a very small faction of the entire company.

Common stock gives no guarantee that you will receive a return of your investment, let alone a dividend. Because common stock carries more risks than preferred stock, it often produces a higher level of return than other types of investments. It sometimes produces great losses as well.

As with debt investments, you also have the option of investing in foreign markets, which does not necessarily mean investing in foreign companies. Just because a company is based in the United States doesn't mean its primary markets are here. Many firms have a significant foreign presence, and much of their planned growth over the next few years will come from their international operations.

Summary and Application

Today's focus has been on preparing for three types of investments. Your best investment is paying off your credit cards. Your next best investment is establishing an emergency fund that will protect you in the case of unexpected expenses. Then you can begin to make other types of investments.

Today we considered several important overarching principles. We considered the need for balance between investing for our own personal needs and investing for eternal significance. We also saw that even small investments will grow exponentially, according to the principle of the time value of money. As well, we learned that we should never invest in assets that carry a higher risk than we can tolerate.

There are a number of types of investments we can make. Some of these investments are fairly complex. Most individuals and couples will be best served if they find a Christian financial advisor they respect and trust who can assist them if they need more complex planning.

Ultimately, the money we invest belongs to God, and the investments we select need to be in accord with the resources God has entrusted to us.

Action Steps for Today

- Determine a payoff schedule for your current credit card debts.
- Establish an emergency fund. Determine a schedule for fully funding it.
- Investigate your employer's 401(k) to determine the availability of a match contribution.
- Find a Christian financial advisor you respect and trust.
- Determine your personal risk tolerance.
- Choose investment strategies that will help you reach your longer term goals.

DAY 7

. . . .

planning for
your future

God created the world in six days, and He rested on the seventh day. You've come to the seventh day of your Money Makeover week, but it's not time to rest until you've considered training your children financially and planning for their future. It may be uncomfortable to think about it, but proper planning for the end of your life cannot be ignored. You could make all the right choices with your money, but if you don't plan for your departure from this world, financial plans you have set for your children can unravel and create significant problems for those who are left behind.

So, don't stop now. You've almost reached the goal of a truly complete money makeover.

. . . .

Training of Our Children

Sons are a heritage from the LORD, children a reward from him (Psalm 127:3).

Children imitate us more than we like to admit. They imitate the words we say (good or bad), our tone of voice, and our food preferences, as well as our deeper, more dearly held values. We should not be surprised that they will imitate how we handle our finances as well. Whether we realize it or not, our children will pick up our attitudes toward money, and discover our true values. They will pick up these habits whether we are providing a good or a bad example—not just when they're teenagers, but beginning when they are very young children.

Training a child to handle money can begin as simply as putting a portion of his or her Christmas money into a bank account and into a weekly church offering. Take your child to the bank with you and explain how a bank works. Elementary-age children can learn that when they deposit money they will earn interest on it. As they grow older, you can explore the concepts of ownership and good stewardship.

When my son Ryan was very young, I tried to explain to him why he needed to place his money in the bank. After a number of frustrating attempts at trying to explain the concept of interest to him, I stated that if he put his $10 in the bank and kept it there for awhile, they would give him $20 back. Ever since then, he has wanted to deposit all of his money in the bank. I guess I should tell him at some point that at the bank's rate of interest it would take 277 years for his money to double! But even if his money never doubles, a penny saved is still a penny earned.

Most of our schools no longer teach the basics of handling finances, such as balancing a checking account or setting up a budget. Whether the school teaches it or not, parents must step up and teach these crucial life skills in a manner that aligns with biblical teachings. Many, many times I've seen parents who have not fulfilled this responsibility and now must bail an adult child out of a major debt, costing significant dollars, time, and hardship.

A few moments spent training your children while they are in your home could save hours or years of heartache later on. Most parents do not take the time to teach these key financial skills because they do not have the skills themselves. That can no longer be said of you now that you have invested seven days to complete your money makeover.

. . . .

Providing the Appropriate Example

Teaching wise and biblical money management takes more than just purchasing a book, even one such as this one. Don't expect your children to read this chapter and become instantly knowledgeable. I hope that, through the concepts that you as a parent learn from this book and then put into practice, you acquire the tools necessary to become an exceptional role model for your child to imitate.

One simple way that you can provide a good example is to talk about your own finances with your children. This can be a touchy subject between parents when one person is more open to sharing this information than the other. Talk with your spouse or other friend (if single) to agree what to say before you have this discussion with your children.

Cultural issues make it difficult for some people to share personal financial information. Others are unsure what age their children should be before they begin to share this information. Some parents have a large amount of assets and don't want their children to assume they can have anything they want just because mom and dad have the money.

On the opposite extreme, parents may be embarrassed to be open because they have managed their finances improperly; they do not wish to look like financial failures to their children.

Regardless of your financial situation, you can confess your individual failures and allow these to act as lessons for your children. Even following the plan discussed throughout this book of getting out of debt and moving toward financial freedom makes you a good role model. Your children will see the changes that you make in your habits and lifestyle and the benefits that can be obtained from financial freedom and a life focused on following God's desires.

. . . .

Giving Our Children Credit Cards

In an age and culture where credit cards—and credit card debt—are so prevalent, many parents wonder: should we give our children a credit card? Recently, I heard one financial planning professional say that it should be illegal for children under age 21 to have a credit card. This may sound a little extreme because, at some point in their lives, your children are going to need to know how to handle credit cards.

Many students go off to college and enter their dorm room to find it very sparsely furnished—except for the credit card application on their desk. Credit card companies spend millions of dollars to leave applications on these desks so they can convince this generation how easy it is to use credit to get the things they want when they want them. Of course, most of these students have already learned this method of immediate gratification before they left home!

I may be one of the few financial planners who actually recommends giving a child a credit card at an earlier age, possibly as early as 16. For those of you who have a 16 year old, this idea may seem insane—but hear me out. Most credit card companies currently offer credit cards with an available credit line of $300 or less. It is important to train your children to use credit cards while they are in your home instead of waiting until they are away from home and alone. This does assume, however, that the parents understand how to use their own credit cards properly.

Credit cards are not the problem; it is the user of the credit cards who creates the problems. It is hard for anyone, given the daily pressures of society and the constant bombardment of advertising, to learn to handle credit cards properly. For a parent, it might be better to lose $300 by paying off a child's credit card when he or she is young rather than having to bail them out later, after they have left home and gotten married, and may have run up as much as a $25,000 credit card balance.

In deciding whether to provide your child a card, it is important to consider two important facts: the child's level of maturity and your ability to provide good counsel in this area. As my children are growing older, this decision is becoming a current reality for me. In my case, I see the way that my children handle money, and I believe they have the maturity necessary to accept this level of responsibility. However, if your children spend everything that comes in when it comes in, you may want to help them understand saving first before providing them the opportunity to have another spending vehicle.

The second issue is what advice you would give them. If you are not managing credit properly, you may not be able to provide this level of training until your financial house is in order. Remember that our children are learning from us and watching us continually.

It is not a matter of "if," but "when" with regard to our children being exposed to credit cards. Without any proper training, they will most likely follow the ways of the world and fall into the temptations that easy money provides for them.

. . . .

Inheritances

Inheritances can be very personal in nature, and thus a wide variety of opinions exist about this topic. For some, the leaving of funds to the children is a normal part of generational aging. Others would rather give their life savings to anyone else before giving any of it to their children.

I know of a wealthy businessman who set up each of his children financially while he was alive, which has allowed him to see the fruits of these investments in his children. However, all future funds will be going to charity and not his children.

Although individuals may not agree on how assets should be dispersed, each family needs to have this conversation because trillions of dollars will be passed down from the current retirees to the Baby Boomers over the next few years.

You've already learned that the current retirees are the generation that saved the most, and the Baby Boomers are the ones who spend the most. The fact is that these funds will be transferred down from the saving generation to the spending generation unless we create legal agreements to the contrary. The Bible can be used to guide us in this area.

> A good man leaves an inheritance for his children's children, but a sinner's wealth is stored up for the righteousness (Proverbs 13:22).

> An inheritance quickly gained at the beginning will not be blessed at the end (Proverbs 20:21).

Although it appears clear that the giving of an inheritance to the next generation is biblical, some parents are often reluctant to give to their kids because of unbiblical lifestyles or spending patterns.

Sometimes I wonder, are these patterns similar to ones learned from the parents? Regardless, the decision of whether to give to children or charities is a personal one.

The bottom line is that you came into this world with nothing, and you are going to leave with nothing. Everything you have will be distributed to others. At that point it becomes a matter of how much and to whom the money is given. By taking the time to plan ahead through wills and trusts, we can at least know that our estate will go to the individuals and organizations that we designate.

If you are concerned about how your children will handle the money in your estate, there is an old but relevant quote that says, "Do your giving while you are living so you are knowing where it is going." This may not seem like an option for those of you who do not know how much money you may need for the rest of your life.

If we start giving small amounts to our children early in life, however, we can observe our children handling the money, see them enjoy it, and further teach them how to handle the money that they will get later in their life.

. . . .

In the Beginning There Is the Will

One of the most basic and important estate documents is the will. The will establishes a number of things, including naming the people to handle your estate when you die, designating who gets specific items of your property, the manner in which your property is to be distributed, and who should take care of any minor children. Often people do not like to think about creating a will because it causes one to realize he or she is not immortal and someday will leave this earth.

The first two sections of a will may not seem to be that important, but the naming of a guardian for your children must not be overlooked. If you do not name a guardian, the courts will step in and name one for you. I know that the guardians we named for our children would probably not be the ones the court would select.

Bottom line: Who do you want making the decision about who raises your children after you die—you or the courts?

. . . .

Health Care Power of Attorney

I am sure that most of us remember the complicated Florida court case concerning Terry Schiavo. The conflict revolved around her last wishes and death. One reason this played out on a national stage was that she had not drafted a health care power of attorney. The health care power of attorney, often overlooked when preparing one's estate, is a relatively simple document.

The health care power of attorney establishes two important things. First, it names the person you would like to make your health care decisions for you if you cannot make them yourself. This could be both a primary person, such as your spouse, and a contingent beneficiary, should the primary person not be able to serve.

Second, it states what your wishes are should you become incapacitated. The usual choices are to keep you alive if at all possible, even if that means keeping you alive by machine, or to pull the plug and allow you to die.

When you make these decisions and have them put into writing, make sure you are using the specific language required by your state. This is one of the reasons to retain the services of an attorney as you prepare these documents.

. . . .

Trusts

Trusts are often a misunderstood part of estate planning. Although this section is not legal instruction, it will provide some basic facts that can help you decide whether or not you need to have a trust.

A trust is a separate estate planning document that does not replace any of the other documents. A trust is a legal document that will determine how your estate is to be settled, what people should be involved in that settlement, who should receive your money, and when they should get the money and other properties.

For some of you, this may sound like the trust does some of the functions of a will; this is partially correct. If you have a trust, you would also have a very simple will that directs that any and all of the assets not titled in the name of the trust be placed in the trust. The major advantage of a trust is that it avoids the costs and time involved with probate. If you have significant assets, a trust enables you to double your allowable exclusion for estate tax purposes, and your heirs thus pay significantly less in estate taxes.

To determine if a trust would be advantageous to you, it is important to consider three things: the assets that would go through probate, the size of your estate, and your family structure. In many cases, people hold assets that would not go through probate, including assets held in retirement or IRA accounts, insurance or annuities, or assets jointly held. In all of these cases, the assets would transfer outside of probate to the beneficiaries or joint owners. If all of your assets would bypass probate, you would not need to create a trust.

The second determining factor is the size of your estate. If you have a sizeable estate of more than a million dollars, a trust may provide you some significant tax advantages. Everyone is currently allowed to transfer certain amounts of money from one generation to another without paying taxes on that transfer. However, the tax laws are constantly changing and the amount that is excluded from tax is also changing.

If you have amounts that exceed the current limits, the tax rates are very high. For some, it may seem like they have worked their entire lives to get ahead only to lose half their estate in taxes when they die. By using separate trusts, you and your spouse each can take advantage of the available estate tax exclusion and save a considerable amount in taxes. However, if you have assets of less than one million dollars, the tax benefits of the trust may not warrant the creation and cost of a trust.

The third area to consider is your family structure. Let me give you an example of a possible estate situation. Let's say you are in a second marriage and each of you has three children (just think of the old television show "The Brady Bunch"). Let's also say that the majority of the assets in the marriage came from the wife as a life insurance settlement from her former husband.

One day the couple was involved in a car accident and the wife was killed instantly, but the husband lived for 30 days before he died. In this case, depending on how their will was written, it could cause all of the wife's assets to be given to the husband upon her death, and upon his death, to his children, completely eliminating all benefits to the wife's children. Although this may be an extreme example, it is something that could and does happen. If you have children from a first marriage and want to ensure that all of your assets go back to your children, a trust may ensure this will happen. If you do not have very many assets and you and your spouse have the same children, it may be more cost effective to create a will instead of the trust.

If you do create a trust, one important reminder is to re-title your assets in the name of the trust, or "fund" your trust by placing assets in it. If you just create the trust document, and do not do anything with the assets of your estate, the effectiveness of the trust will be lost.

. . . .

Do We Need an Attorney?

There are a number of ways that a will can be created. You may handwrite a will, often called a holographic will; you can use a template that can be obtained on the Internet or through software programs or books; or you can hire the services of an attorney.

Although an attorney can be costly, there is often a significant benefit in using an attorney. When you draw up other legal documents, if something is not stated correctly it can later be revised. However, if there are problems with a will or if the document you produced proves to be invalid, this would not be found out until after you die. Unfortunately, you cannot change the document after that occurs.

As well, there is state-related terminology that is required for the will to be valid within the state in which you live. Although I usually suggest avoiding spending money, creating a valid will is one of those times when it is a wise to spend some money. Fortunately, it usually does not cost any extra to hire an estate planning attorney who is a specialist in this area rather than just choosing an attorney who generally deals with commercial documents or corporate actions.

An estate planning attorney focuses on just wills and trusts, so he or she is an expert in this area. As tax laws change frequently, it is important to find a person who keeps up with these changes and can be creative with how the estate is handled.

An attorney usually charges by the hour, so it is important to do the homework up front regarding how your estate is to be handled. Here are some questions that should be answered before going to an attorney:

1. Are there any specific personal items that you would like to go to any individuals?

2. Who do you want to take care of your affairs after you die? Who would be the contingent people in case these people would be unwilling to serve?

3. Who would you want to take care of your minor children if you were to die or become incapacitated? If they are unwilling, who would you select as a contingent care provider?

4. What powers do you want to give your personal representative?

As you review these considerations, draw up a comprehensive list of possible answers to these questions, and then make sure you update your will every few years.

Someone you named many years ago may no longer be able to perform the services that you request. In some cases, he or she may have died. I have known some cases in which the couple had divorced, and a family member of the divorced spouse was named as executor. This obviously caused significant relationship problems as the estate and guardianship were settled.

. . . .

Understanding God's Calling in Our Lives

We are all on earth for a purpose. Author Rick Warren calls us to look at our individual lives as purpose driven. We are here to fulfill the purpose for which God created us. A part of this calling means using our financial resources in service to God and others.

Have we already fulfilled God's calling on our lives? If we had already completed our work for God, there would be little reason for us to remain on earth. God would already have called us to heaven.

Make sure that you have given thoughtful planning and are financially prepared so that you can fulfill the purposes that God has for you while you are alive and even after you leave this earth. I imagine entering heaven only to discover missed opportunities to use my finances to help others, to support relationships, to provide for that person down the street, or to bring that brother or sister into the kingdom of God.

What an exciting opportunity to look for this purpose in our lives, and then to act on it when the time comes! God is working through each of us to extend His kingdom.

We need to start living each day of our lives as an opportunity for service to God. Can we personally make this change of attitude? Can we move from where we are now to a renewed level of excitement and service?

I believe that we can all move in this direction if we focus on the power, not of this world, but of Christ Jesus.

Summary and Application

Each of the documents listed in this section brings us very close to the reality that we will not be living on earth forever, and that we need to appropriately prepare for the day of our departure. There are some very specific steps that one needs to take to make sure that one's affairs and documents are taken care of promptly.

Action Steps for Today

- Determine the areas in which you still need to train up your children in the area of finances. Take specific action, regardless of their age, to train them in these areas.
- Review your estate plan to make sure that you have current and up-to-date documents. If not, make an appointment with an attorney to revise them.

. . . .

appendices

Worksheet 1: Variable Income and Expenses

Periodic Income Payments

	Annual Amount	Monthly Amount
Bonuses – Primary	_____	_____
Bonuses – Secondary	_____	_____
Income Tax Refunds	_____	_____
Other _____	_____	_____
Other _____	_____	_____
	Total Monthly:	_____

Periodic Expense Payments

	Annual Amount	Monthly Amount
Insurances: Auto	_____	_____
Medical: Doctors	_____	_____
Medical: Dentists	_____	_____
Birthday Presents	_____	_____
Christmas Presents	_____	_____
Property Taxes	_____	_____
Children's School Expenses	_____	_____
Vacations	_____	_____
Other _____	_____	_____
Other _____	_____	_____
Other _____	_____	_____
	Total Monthly:	_____

Worksheet 2: Monthly Income and Expenses

Monthly Income

Primary _____

Secondary _____

Other Income _____

Total Monthly Income _____

Monthly Expenses

Taxes (Fed/State/FICA) _____

Housing _____

Communications (Tele/Internet/Cell) _____

Utilities _____

Home: Maintenance/Fees _____

Housing: Other Expenses _____

Giving to Others (Charitable Giving) _____

Food _____

Insurances _____

Auto/s _____

Debt/Credit Card Payments _____

Hobbies _____

Entertainment _____

Vacations _____

Children/Childcare _____

Medical _____

Clothing _____

Savings _____

Miscellaneous Expenses _____

Monthly Variable Expenses (Worksheet 1) _____

Total Monthly Expenses: _____

The Bottom Line (+/-): _____

(Monthly Income Minus Expenses)

Worksheet 3: Balance Sheet

Assets (Things That You Own)

Item	Current value:
Checking Accounts	_____
Savings Accounts	_____
Investment Accounts	_____
Retirement Accounts	_____
Cash Value of Life Insurance	_____
Home	_____
Autos	_____
Jewelry	_____
Other _____	_____
Other _____	_____
Total Household Assets:	_____

Debts (Things That You Owe)

Total from Debt Listing Worksheet _____

Net Worth: _____

Note: Take the total assets and subtract total debts to arrive at your net worth.

Worksheet 4: Debt Listing Worksheet

Outstanding Bills	Rate	Current Balance
_____	_____	_____
_____	_____	_____
_____	_____	_____
_____	_____	_____
Credit Card 1	_____	_____
Credit Card 2	_____	_____
Auto 1	_____	_____
Auto 2	_____	_____
Home Mortgage	_____	_____
Second Mortgage	_____	_____
Other _____	_____	_____
Other _____	_____	_____
Other _____	_____	_____
Other _____	_____	_____
Other _____	_____	_____
Other _____	_____	_____
Other _____	_____	_____
Other _____	_____	_____
Other _____	_____	_____

Total Debts: _____

Worksheet 5: Absolutes/Non-Absolutes

Single Person/Husband Absolutes

_____

_____

_____

_____

_____

_____

_____

_____

_____

_____

Wife Absolutes

_____

_____

_____

_____

_____

_____

_____

_____

_____

_____

Single Person/Husband Non-Absolutes

_____

_____

_____

_____

_____

_____

_____

_____

_____

Wife Non-Absolutes

_____

_____

_____

_____

_____

_____

_____

_____

_____

Worksheet 6: Ideas for Balancing the Budget

Expense Item	Action That Can Be Taken	Potential Monthly Savings
_____	_____	_____
_____	_____	_____
_____	_____	_____
_____	_____	_____
_____	_____	_____
_____	_____	_____
_____	_____	_____
_____	_____	_____
_____	_____	_____
_____	_____	_____
_____	_____	_____
_____	_____	_____
_____	_____	_____
_____	_____	_____
_____	_____	_____
_____	_____	_____
_____	_____	_____

Total Potential Monthly Savings: _____

Worksheet 7: Budget Development Form

Monthly Income	Current	Changes	New Budget	Percent
Primary	_____	_____	_____	_____
Secondary	_____	_____	_____	_____
Other Income	_____	_____	_____	_____
Total Monthly Income	_____	_____	_____	_____
Monthly Expenses				
Taxes (Fed/State/FICA)	_____	_____	_____	_____
Housing	_____	_____	_____	_____
Communications (Tele/Internet/Cell)	_____	_____	_____	_____
Utilities	_____	_____	_____	_____
Home: Maintenance/Fees	_____	_____	_____	_____
Housing: Other Expenses	_____	_____	_____	_____
Giving to Others	_____	_____	_____	_____
Food	_____	_____	_____	_____
Insurances	_____	_____	_____	_____
Auto/s	_____	_____	_____	_____
Debt/Credit Card Payments	_____	_____	_____	_____
Hobbies	_____	_____	_____	_____
Entertainment	_____	_____	_____	_____
Vacations	_____	_____	_____	_____
Children/Childcare	_____	_____	_____	_____
Medical	_____	_____	_____	_____
Clothing	_____	_____	_____	_____
Savings	_____	_____	_____	_____
Miscellaneous Expenses	_____	_____	_____	_____
Monthly Variable Expenses (Worksheet 1)	_____	_____	_____	_____
Total Monthly Expenses:	_____	_____	_____	_____
The Bottom Line (+/-):	_____	_____	_____	_____

(Monthly Income Minus the Expenses)

Worksheet 8: Check Allocation Form

Monthly Income	Percentage from Budget	Allocation
Primary	_____	_____
Secondary	_____	_____
Other Income	_____	_____
Total Monthly Income:	_____	_____

Monthly Expenses		
Taxes (Fed/State/FICA)	_____	_____
Housing	_____	_____
Communications (Tele/Internet/Cell)	_____	_____
Utilities	_____	_____
Home: Maintenance/Fees	_____	_____
Housing: Other Expenses	_____	_____
Giving to Others	_____	_____
Food	_____	_____
Insurances	_____	_____
Auto/s	_____	_____
Debt/Credit Card Payments	_____	_____
Hobbies	_____	_____
Entertainment	_____	_____
Vacations	_____	_____
Children/Childcare	_____	_____
Medical	_____	_____
Clothing	_____	_____
Savings	_____	_____
Miscellaneous Expenses	_____	_____
Monthly Variable Expenses (Worksheet 1)	_____	_____
Total Allocations:	_____	_____

Worksheet 9: Individual Account Pages

Income/Expense Category: _____   **Budgeted Monthly Amt:** _____

Date	Check No.	Paid to	Increase	Decrease	Balance
____	_____	_____	_____	_____	_____
____	_____	_____	_____	_____	_____
____	_____	_____	_____	_____	_____
____	_____	_____	_____	_____	_____
____	_____	_____	_____	_____	_____
____	_____	_____	_____	_____	_____
____	_____	_____	_____	_____	_____
____	_____	_____	_____	_____	_____
____	_____	_____	_____	_____	_____
____	_____	_____	_____	_____	_____
____	_____	_____	_____	_____	_____
____	_____	_____	_____	_____	_____
____	_____	_____	_____	_____	_____
____	_____	_____	_____	_____	_____
____	_____	_____	_____	_____	_____
____	_____	_____	_____	_____	_____
____	_____	_____	_____	_____	_____
____	_____	_____	_____	_____	_____
____	_____	_____	_____	_____	_____
____	_____	_____	_____	_____	_____
____	_____	_____	_____	_____	_____
____	_____	_____	_____	_____	_____

Worksheet 10: Personal Spending Register

Date	Check No.	Paid to	Category	Amount
——	——————	——————	———————	————
——	——————	——————	———————	————
——	——————	——————	———————	————
——	——————	——————	———————	————
——	——————	——————	———————	————
——	——————	——————	———————	————
——	——————	——————	———————	————
——	——————	——————	———————	————
——	——————	——————	———————	————
——	——————	——————	———————	————
——	——————	——————	———————	————
——	——————	——————	———————	————
——	——————	——————	———————	————
——	——————	——————	———————	————
——	——————	——————	———————	————
——	——————	——————	———————	————
——	——————	——————	———————	————
——	——————	——————	———————	————
——	——————	——————	———————	————
——	——————	——————	———————	————
——	——————	——————	———————	————
——	——————	——————	———————	————

Worksheet 11: Account Savings Page

Savings Category

Savings Category	Beginning Amt	Alloc_	Final Amt	Ending Balance
Housing				
Communications (Tele/Internet/Cell)				
Utilities				
Home: Maintenance/Fees				
Housing: Other Expenses				
Giving to Others				
Food				
Insurances				
Auto/s				
Debt/Credit Card Payments				
Hobbies				
Entertainment				
Vacations				

Savings Category p. 2

	Beginning Amt	Alloc_	Final Amt	Ending Balance
Children/Child Care				
Medical				
Clothing				
Savings				
Miscellaneous Expenses				
Monthly Variable Expenses (Worksheet 1)				
Total Savings:				

Worksheet 12: Checking Account Reconciliation

Current Balance of All Savings Account Categories _____

Balance of Current Month Individual Account Pages _____

Total Balances: _____

Add: Uncleared Items from Individual Account Pages _____

Total Household Balance: _____

Bank Statement Balance: _____

Difference: _____

Worksheet 13: List of Goals

Goal Area	Specific Goal
_____	_____
_____	_____
_____	_____
_____	_____
_____	_____
_____	_____
_____	_____
_____	_____
_____	_____
_____	_____
_____	_____
_____	_____
_____	_____
_____	_____
_____	_____
_____	_____
_____	_____
_____	_____
_____	_____
_____	_____

Worksheet 14: Goal Development Form

Priority   **Goal Area**   **Specific Goal**

_____   _____   _____

Potential Obstacles to Achieving Goal: _____

Goal Timetable: _____

Accountability Person: _____

Action Steps

1) _____

2) _____

3) _____

Priority   **Goal Area**   **Specific Goal**

_____   _____   _____

Potential Obstacles to Achieving Goal: _____

Goal Timetable: _____

Accountability Person: _____

Action Steps

1) _____

2) _____

3) _____

Priority **Goal Area** **Specific Goal**

_____ _____ _____

Potential Obstacles to Achieving Goal: _____

Goal Timetable: _____

Accountability Person: _____

Action Steps

1) _____

2) _____

3) _____

Priority **Goal Area** **Specific Goal**

_____ _____ _____

Potential Obstacles to Achieving Goal: _____

Goal Timetable: _____

Accountability Person: _____

Action Steps

1) _____

2) _____

3) _____

Priority **Goal Area** **Specific Goal**

_____ _____ _____

Potential Obstacles to Achieving Goal: _____

Goal Timetable: _____

Accountability Person: _____

Action Steps

1) _____

2) _____

3) _____

book group
discussion questions

Group Discussion Questions — Introduction

- Entering this seven-day process, how do you honestly feel? Are you excited about this process, or are you apprehensive?
- What would it mean for you to not have the continual stresses of financial issues in your life?
- At this point in the process, do you believe that you can remove the stress of finances within your life?
- At this point in the process, what would prevent you from taking actions with your finances?
- How many other people in this country do you believe share the same level of financial issues and problems as you do?
- Where/from whom did you learn about the process of money management? Was this person a good or poor example for you?
- Does it surprise you that guidance for our financial lives can come from the Bible?
- What do you believe caused the American public to move so far away from the use of biblical principles to manage our finances?
- What is the worst financial decision that you have made in the past?
- When was the last time that you spent money on yourself in an almost selfish manner?

. . . .

Group Discussion Questions — Day 1

- What are some of the ways in which you have tried to "keep up with the Joneses" in the past?
- What did you learn about yourself when you completed the variable expense worksheet and the monthly income and expense worksheet?
- In looking at your overall level of debt, how do you feel?
- How does looking at your current income in relation to the income of many other parts of the world make you feel?
- As you look at your overall monthly surplus or deficit, or your overall net worth, what are some things that you can learn from this process?

. . . .

Group Discussion Questions — Day 2

- What are some ways in which you have seen mismanagement of God's resources by others? How about yourself?
- Why is it so hard to accept that God is the true owner of all of our possessions?
- In what ways can you demonstrate your stewardship of the possessions that God has given you?
- Discuss in your group the following statement: God may withhold resources from you if you are not managing your resources properly.
- When we say that God is the true owner of everything, how does this concept relate to our children and who they belong to?
- Can you remember a purchase that you made in the past that you had wanted for some time but that left you with an empty feeling inside after you had purchased it?
- What does it mean to be satisfied with the possessions that you have?
- How do we go about changing our attitudes about money?
- Why is it so difficult to establish the right balance in our lives?
- Who are those who are truly wealthy in this life?

. . . .

Group Discussion Questions — Day 3

- What are some techniques that could prevent disagreements between you and your spouse as you go through this process of identifying the spending changes that are necessary?
- What would your life be like without television, cable, or cell phones? Would it "drive you nuts" or would it be a freeing experience?
- What do you think about the suggestions for groceries, restaurants and clothing as possible options for your family?
- How difficult was it for you to identify areas of your life where spending could change?
- What was your greatest struggle, both in balancing your budget and in creating margin in your budget?
- Which of the effective budgeting keys were especially helpful to you? Which of them were the least helpful?
- If you are married, what are some techniques you have used to create harmony with your spouse?
- Is there any area of your life that you would still consider excessive after going though the exercises of today?
- Which budgeting system did you select? Has it been a success or failure since you implemented it?
- Who is (or who will be) your accountability partner as you work through this process?

Group Discussion Questions — Day 4

- Do you believe that debt is good or bad for the American consumer? What about the debts of governments, which are used to support their people? Are there any biblical references you can cite for guidance?
- Review some of the differences that you see between the spending patterns of males and females.
- What are some ways in which you can avoid the lure of consumer advertising and pleas from marketers for increased consumption?
- Is a reduction in consumer spending un-American?
- Do you think that you could purchase a car for cash?
- Have you used credit cards effectively in the past? Where have you experienced problems with credit cards in the past?
- From your perspective, what are some ways that you could reduce your health care spending?
- Why do we seem to need larger and larger homes today?
- What are your current attitudes toward autos? Are these proper attitudes from a biblical perspective?
- Do you think, after reading this section, that leasing is still a good way to purchase a car?
- What are your attitudes toward the lottery? What about the other forms of gambling? As a Christian, do you believe that we should participate in such activities?
- What are some things you need to do differently based on the knowledge that you have gained in this area?

. . . .

Group Discussion Questions — Day 5

- How does the creation of goals fit into your overall financial plan?
- Based on the various categories of goals, which ones were the easiest for you to create?
- Why does it seem so hard to take the necessary time to spend in the Word or in devotion to God?
- What are some ways that we can free up some time to spend in the Word and in personal devotion?
- Are you satisfied with the career that you chose? As markets become more global, how stable will this career be for you in the future?
- If you could have any career today, what would you want to do? What would be your perfect job?
- Cite examples of situations in which your friends have been there for you.
- What are some methods that you use to stay in touch with your friends?
- In spite of the readily available information on good nutrition, why is it that people are growing continually larger? Why is this the case with our children?
- How are you saving for your retirement? Do you think what you are doing will be enough?
- How do you think retirement will be different for you than it was for your parents?
- Do you believe that you can become debt free in this life?

Group Discussion Questions — Day 6

- What does the concept of investing based on biblical principles mean to you?
- How can we find a balance between earthly and eternal savings?
- In what ways are you focusing your time and energy toward becoming wealthy in this life?
- Is it a sin today to be rich?
- What are some investments you have made in the past that have performed exceptionally well? What are some investments that have performed poorly? How was each of these investments chosen?
- What is your level of understanding of today's financial markets? Has this helped or hindered you with investing in some of these markets?
- Do you believe that you can beat the markets with appropriate investments over a longer period of time (do you favor a passive or active investment approach)?
- Should Christians invest their resources in today's financial markets?
- What do you need to work on to gain a better understanding of the financial benefits provided by your employer?

. . . .

Group Discussion Questions — Day 7

- Can you remember specific times when your parents trained you in the handling of money?
- What are some ways that we can set an appropriate example for our children in the area of finances?
- What methods have you used in the training of your children on how to handle money?
- What do you think about giving your child a credit card? Do you think you have the ability to train them properly on how to use one?
- Why are we as Christians so reluctant to talk about our eventual deaths? Will that not be a time of rejoicing for us?
- What is your particular household's view on inheritances? Where do you think many of those views came from?
- Based on your review of your estate documents, what changes were required?
- Respond to this question: God is not finished with me yet!

Group Discussion Questions — Conclusion

- What is preventing you from making the changes that are necessary in your financial life today?
- What specific actions are you going to take today after working through this book?

. . . .

References

Gibson, R. C. (1990). *Asset Allocation: Balancing Financial Risk.* Burr Ridge, IL: Irwin Professional Publishing.

Gire, P. J. (2008). Between the issues: Missing the ten best. *Journal of Financial Planning, 1*, 1.

....

internet resources

Enjoy these free web supplements and tools to maximize your seven-day experience!

As an added resource as you complete this book, here are several additional forms and articles to help you put your financial house in order. Go to *www.sevendaymakeover.com* now to access these FREE additional resources, which including:

- All of the worksheets in Word and Excel format
- Quick retirement planner
- Understanding financial markets
- Recommended investment strategies
- How can I purchase my first investment?
- Setting up your first brokerage account
- Understanding life insurance
- Financial accounts for children
- Selecting an investment advisor
- Understanding financial designations

195

about the author

Eric Hoogstra is associate professor of business at Cornerstone University in Grand Rapids, Michigan.

In addition to this full time role, he is an adjunct professor at Grand Valley State University and Indiana Wesleyan University. He also serves as a seminar instructor for Crown Financial Ministries and a corporate facilitator for Dave Ramsey's Financial Peace University.

Eric received his Bachelor's of Science in Business Administration (BSBA) in 1985, a Master's of Business Administration (MBA) in finance in 1989, and a doctor of philosophy (Ph.D.) in management in 2007.

In addition to his teaching, he is involved with a number of companies in the financial, consulting, real estate, and manufacturing industries.

Eric's certification marks include the CFP® (Certified Financial Planner), ChFC (Chartered Financial Consultant), CLU (Chartered Life Underwriter), and a CM (Certified Manager). He is an NASD registered representative licensed through G.A. Repple, where he maintains multiple security and insurance licenses.

Eric is a lifelong resident of Western Michigan and serves in a variety of capacities within his church and throughout the community.

Eric resides in Zeeland, Michigan, with his wife Ranae, son Ryan, and daughter Lindsey.